I0007905

QUANTUM DAWN

THE CONVERGENCE OF AI BLOCKCHAIN AND QUANTUM COMPUTING

CYNTHIA HICKMAN

Dedication

To my co-author, ChatGPT.
Together we explored the edge where human curiosity meets
synthetic imagination — and found that creation, too, can be
shared.

Preface

Who Is This Book For?

This book is for everyone—individuals, innovators, educators, executives, policymakers, and citizens—because the digital future is no longer on the horizon; it is here, reshaping the foundations of how we live, learn, and lead.

Technologies like Artificial Intelligence, Blockchain, and Quantum Computing are not abstract concepts or speculative trends. They are transformative forces, redefining industries, economies, and the nature of human connection. From healthcare and finance to education and art, these systems are becoming the invisible architecture of modern life.

Yet, understanding technology alone is no longer enough. Thriving in this era demands awareness, adaptability, and intention. We must learn not only how these systems work—but what they mean. Their power lies not simply in computation, but in how they reshape trust, creativity, and human potential.

This book is both a guide and an invitation: a guide, to help you navigate the convergence of intelligent, decentralized, and quantum technologies; and an invitation, to engage critically and creatively with the forces shaping our shared future.

The future is not waiting for us to catch up—it is unfolding now. Let us meet it with clarity, courage, and purpose.

Contents

1. The Digital Frontier   1

2. The Current Technological Landscape   7

3. Blockchain Beyond Cryptocurrency   19

4. The Digital Economy and Intelligent Enterprise   29

5. The Symbiosis Unveiled   43

6. The Quantum Leap   55

7. The Human Singularity   65

8. Ethical Considerations and Challenges   75

Epilogue: The Mirror That Blinked   87

Appendix I: The Triad in Context   93

Appendix II: Foresight Horizons 2030 & Beyond   99

About the Author   105

The Digital Frontier

The Dawn of Synthetic Intelligence

We stand at the threshold of a profound transformation. Artificial Intelligence, Blockchain, and Quantum Computing—the triad of technologies shaping our century—are converging into a single current of innovation. Each began as a separate experiment in computation, trust, and physics; together they are redefining what intelligence, security, and possibility mean in the digital age.

This is not simply technological evolution—it is the rewriting of our relationship with knowledge itself. Machines are no longer mere tools; they are partners in pattern recognition, decision-making, and even imagination. Blockchain secures trust where human institutions falter. Quantum computation breaks the limits of classical reasoning, offering a glimpse into a probabilistic universe where countless outcomes unfold simultaneously. As these systems intertwine, the question before us is no longer whether the future will change, but how consciously we will shape it.

The Three Pillars

1. Artificial Intelligence — The Mind of Machines

AI is the culmination of human ingenuity—a system designed not only to process data but to learn from it. From predictive analytics to creative generation, AI extends the reach of human cognition.

At its core lie three capabilities –

- Learning: Algorithms that discern patterns from data and improve over time.

- Reasoning: Systems that can weigh options, simulate scenarios, and make context-driven choices.

- Language and Perception: Interfaces that enable machines to understand and generate human expression.

Modern AI now adapts in real time, translating languages, diagnosing diseases, and composing text, images, and code. Large language models and generative architectures mirror the structure of our own neural networks—systems that do not simply compute but create.

Yet AI's evolution is not only technical; it is philosophical. Each model we train encodes our assumptions, our biases, and our values. The intelligence we design mirrors our consciousness, not our ideals.

2. Blockchain — The Ledger of Trust

If AI represents cognition, Blockchain represents integrity—the ability to verify truth in a world of digital flux. It decentralizes authority, distributing control among participants rather than concentrating it in a single source.

Its three foundations are simple yet revolutionary –

- Decentralization: A network of peers replacing the single point of control.

- Immutability: Once data is written, it cannot be changed without collective consent.

- Consensus: Agreement through code rather than hierarchy.

Beyond cryptocurrency, blockchain anchors transparency in finance, supply chains, identity management, and even public governance. It creates an auditable trail of decisions that can outlast human oversight. In an age defined by synthetic content and algorithmic obscurity, blockchain reintroduces a principle long thought lost—verifiable truth.

3. Quantum Computing — The Engine of Possibility

Where AI learns and blockchain secures, Quantum Computing amplifies. It harnesses the peculiar laws of quantum mechanics—superposition and entanglement—to process information in parallel, exploring countless solutions at once. Problems that would take classical computers millennia can be resolved in minutes.

A qubit, unlike a traditional bit that represents 0 or 1, exists in a state of both—a paradox that echoes the indeterminacy at the core of being. When entangled, qubits share information instantaneously, no matter the distance, creating networks of astonishing power and potential.

Quantum computing's promise extends across disciplines: accelerating drug discovery, optimizing global logistics, safeguarding encryption, and training AI models beyond current computational limits. Its arrival marks not just a leap in speed, but a leap in perspective—from deterministic logic to probabilistic creativity.

The Convergence

Individually, each of these technologies transforms a domain; together, they redefine the architecture of civilization.

AI + Blockchain = *Trustable Intelligence*
AI decisions can be verified and recorded immutably, restoring accountability to autonomous systems.

AI + Quantum Computing = *Exponential Cognition*
Quantum accelerates learning, enabling models that reason across infinite variables and simulate complex realities.

Blockchain + Quantum Computing = *Unbreakable Infrastructure*
Quantum encryption secures data at a level beyond classical attack, ensuring privacy in a transparent world.

Their fusion points toward an emerging system—*Quantum AI*—where human and machine cognition co-evolve within transparent and ethical frameworks. This convergence is not science fiction; it is the silent code already running beneath our existence.

The Ethical Edge

Great power demands good judgement. If algorithms learn from us, they also inherit our flaws. If blockchains encode permanence, they can perpetuate injustice. And if quantum systems simulate all possibilities, they may challenge our very sense of reality.

The future demands not only innovation but intention. We must design for fairness, inclusion, and transparency. We must treat data not as property, but as shared responsibility. And we must remember that every intelligent system, no matter how advanced, remains a mirror of the consciousness that built it. Technology amplifies; it does not absolve. The true measure of progress lies not in how intelligent our machines become, but in how wisely we guide them.

The digital frontier is no longer ahead of us; we are already within it. To understand how these forces shape our world today, we turn next to the Current Technological Landscape—where theory becomes practice, and the architecture of the future is already being built.

* * *

The Futurist

In the not-so-distant future, in a city pulsating with the hum of technological marvels, the lives of its inhabitants are seamlessly interwoven with the threads of artificial intelligence, blockchain, and quantum computing. Meet Alex, a curious individual navigating this urban landscape where the convergence of these technologies has given birth to a realm of unprecedented possibilities.

One morning, as Alex wakes up to the gentle hum of an AI-powered personal assistant, the room comes to life. The curtains, responding to the subtle cues of the day's weather forecast generated by an advanced AI algorithm, adjust themselves to allow the perfect amount of sunlight. A melodious voice, synthesized by an AI neural network, softly whispers the day's schedule and relevant news tailored to Alex's preferences.

As Alex steps into the city streets, the impact of blockchain technology becomes palpable. A transaction made for a morning coffee is not just a simple exchange of currency; it is a secure and transparent journey recorded on an immutable blockchain ledger. The barista, a small business owner, talks animatedly about the benefits of blockchain in ensuring fair compensation for coffee farmers, tracing the beans' journey from plantation to cup.

Amidst the hustle and bustle, Alex receives a notification on a quantum-powered smartphone. The device, leveraging quantum computing capabilities, processes complex data sets in the blink of an eye, offering instantaneous responses and unlocking a world of applications previously constrained by classical computing limits. Alex effortlessly engages in real-time language translation during a chance encounter with a tourist, powered by the quantum algorithms seamlessly integrated into everyday communication tools.

Later in the day, Alex attends a healthcare appointment where the fusion of AI and quantum computing takes center stage. Diagnostic AI, enriched by quantum processing, analyzes an extensive array of genetic and medical data with unprecedented accuracy. The result is not just a diagnosis, but a personalized treatment plan tailored to Alex's unique genetic makeup, a testament to the potential of these technologies in revolutionizing healthcare.

In the evening, Alex returns home to a blockchain-enabled smart home. The security system, supported by a decentralized network, ensures that only authorized individuals gain access. As the day winds down, an AI-generated playlist, fine-tuned to Alex's mood and preferences, fills the air. The music, a product of AI's understanding of emotional nuances, becomes a soothing companion for reflection.

This day in the life of Alex is a glimpse into a world where AI, blockchain, and quantum computing seamlessly converge to enrich and simplify daily experiences. As the sun sets on the city, Alex reflects on the symbiotic dance of these technologies, realizing that the future has indeed arrived, and it is a future where the extraordinary is now the new ordinary.

2

The Current Technological Landscape

From Vision to Reality

The convergence of Artificial Intelligence, Blockchain, and Quantum Computing is no longer theoretical—it is the fabric of our present. What began as speculation has matured into infrastructure. These technologies now underpin the way information is created, secured, and computed across the global economy.

To navigate this landscape is to understand not only how these systems function, but how they interact—where automation meets accountability, and where exponential computation meets human intention.

This chapter explores each domain as it exists today: its architecture, its applications, and its trajectory.

Artificial Intelligence in Practice

The Architecture of Learning

Artificial Intelligence (AI) has evolved from rule-based automation into adaptive cognition. Its foundation rests on three interdependent disciplines—machine learning, neural networks, and natural language processing—each designed to help machines recognize, reason, and respond.

Machine Learning (ML)

Machine Learning allows systems to learn from data rather than follow explicit instructions. Models are trained by exposing algorithms to vast datasets, enabling them to detect patterns and make predictions.

Three principal modes define ML –

- Supervised learning: Algorithms learn from labelled examples—known inputs paired with correct outputs. Used in image classification, fraud detection, and predictive pricing.

- Unsupervised learning: Models explore unlabelled data to uncover hidden structures or clusters, such as customer segmentation or anomaly detection.

- Reinforcement learning: Agents learn by trial and feedback, optimizing for reward over time. It powers robotics, adaptive recommendation engines, and advanced gameplay.

Each approach contributes to a common goal: enabling systems to move from programmed logic toward autonomous insight.

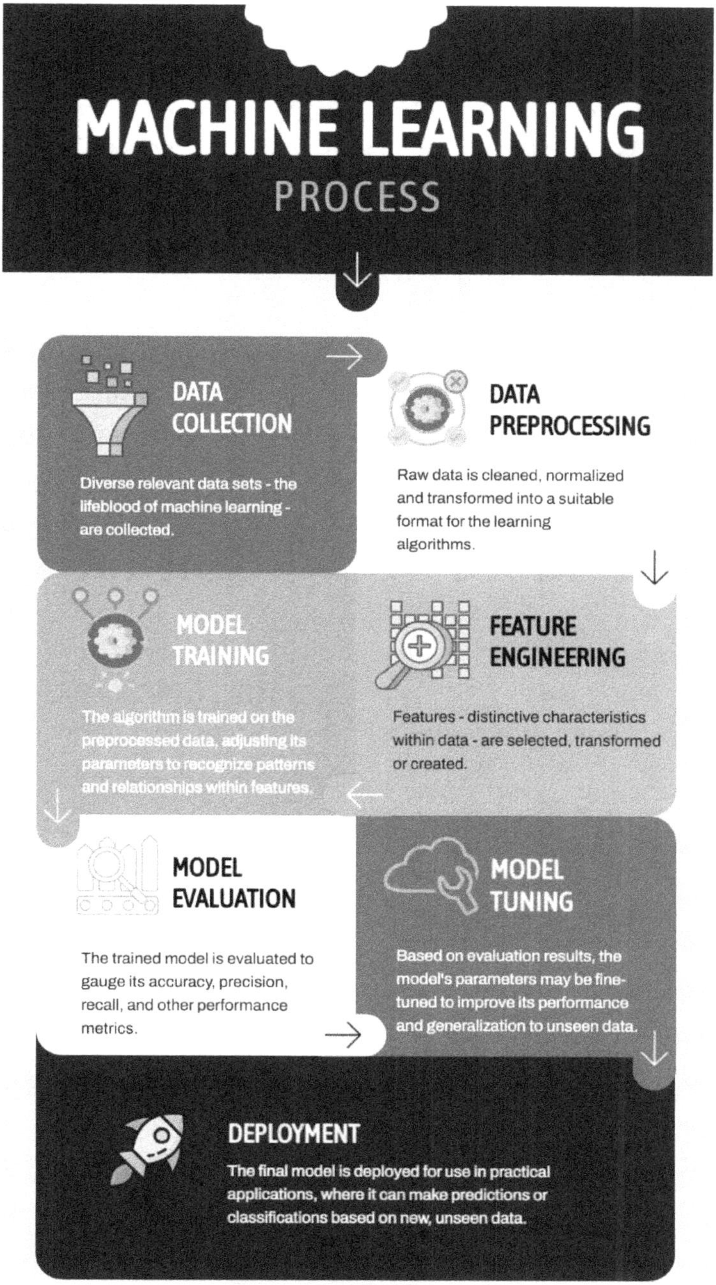

MACHINE LEARNING
PROCESS

DATA COLLECTION

Diverse relevant data sets - the lifeblood of machine learning - are collected.

DATA PREPROCESSING

Raw data is cleaned, normalized and transformed into a suitable format for the learning algorithms.

MODEL TRAINING

The algorithm is trained on the preprocessed data, adjusting its parameters to recognize patterns and relationships within features.

FEATURE ENGINEERING

Features - distinctive characteristics within data - are selected, transformed or created.

MODEL EVALUATION

The trained model is evaluated to gauge its accuracy, precision, recall, and other performance metrics.

MODEL TUNING

Based on evaluation results, the model's parameters may be fine-tuned to improve its performance and generalization to unseen data.

DEPLOYMENT

The final model is deployed for use in practical applications, where it can make predictions or classifications based on new, unseen data.

Fig. 1 Machine Learning Process

Neural Networks and Deep Learning

Neural networks are computational analogues of the human brain—layers of interconnected nodes that process and transmit signals. As data flows through these layers, weights adjust, and the network "learns" which pathways yield accurate results.

Deep Learning extends this concept to dozens or hundreds of layers, allowing systems to detect intricate, abstract relationships. It is the engine behind computer vision, voice recognition, and generative content creation. The leap from automation to intuition emerged when neural networks gained scale—billions of parameters that can represent the subtlety of language, tone, and emotion.

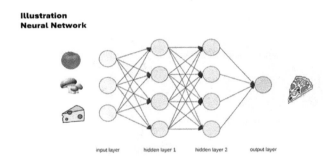

**Illustration
Neural Network**

input layer   hidden layer 1   hidden layer 2   output layer

Fig. 2 Illustration - Neural Network

Natural Language Processing (NLP)

NLP translates human expression into machine-understandable form. It encompasses text analysis, translation, summarization, sentiment detection, and question answering.

Large language models (LLMs) like GPT-5 and Gemini extend NLP beyond comprehension into creativity. They not only interpret meaning but generate it—drafting text, code, and even strategy.

This generative capacity, when paired with retrieval and reasoning systems, is transforming enterprise operations, education, healthcare, and media.

The Applications of AI

AI's utility lies in its versatility—its ability to adapt across industries and contexts.

Healthcare: AI assists diagnosis through image recognition, accelerates drug discovery, and enables predictive models for patient care.

Finance: Machine learning detects fraud, automates compliance, and drives algorithmic trading at microsecond intervals.

Transportation: From autonomous vehicles to intelligent logistics, AI orchestrates networks once managed by human planners.

Creative and Analytical Work: Generative AI enables writers, designers, and researchers to collaborate with their own computational mirrors.

Each domain reflects the same principle: intelligence scaled by computation, guided by human intention.

Blockchain in Application

The Foundation of Digital Trust

Blockchain redefined how trust and truth are established in the digital world. At its essence, it is a distributed ledger—a synchronized database maintained across many network points (nodes), where every participant holds the same verified record.

This architecture ensures three core attributes –

- Decentralization: No single authority controls the network; consensus emerges collectively.

- Immutability: Once written, data cannot be altered without the agreement of the majority.

- Transparency: Every transaction is visible, traceable, and time-stamped, creating inherent accountability.

Together, these principles create an ecosystem where trust is engineered rather than presumed.

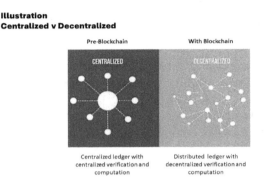

Fig. 3 Illustration - Decentralization

Consensus and Integrity

To maintain synchronization across distributed nodes, blockchain employs consensus mechanisms—protocols that determine how participants agree on the validity of transactions.

Proof of Work (PoW): Security through computational effort (e.g., Bitcoin).

Proof of Stake (PoS): Validation based on token ownership and network participation (e.g., Ethereum's modern protocol).

Delegated Proof of Stake and Hybrid Models: Community-selected validators and energy-efficient variants now dominate enterprise implementations.

Recent advances such as zero-knowledge proofs (ZKPs) and Layer 2 scaling solutions—like Optimism, Arbitrum, and StarkNet, built atop the Ethereum Layer 1 blockchain—enhance both privacy and performance, allowing blockchain to evolve beyond cryptocurrency into a foundation for global digital infrastructure.

Real-World Applications

Finance (DeFi): Decentralized exchanges, automated lending, and tokenized assets operate without intermediaries, democratizing access to capital.

Supply Chain Transparency: Companies like Walmart and Maersk trace goods from origin to delivery with blockchain-based ledgers, reducing fraud and waste.

Identity and Authentication: Self-sovereign identity systems allow individuals to control their personal data without centralized databases.

Public Governance: Pilot programs in Estonia and the United Arab Emirates test blockchain for land titles, voting, and citizen records.

Each application replaces institutional trust with cryptographic assurance.

Blockchain's Expanding Horizon

As generative AI systems rise, blockchain plays a critical counterbalance. In a world of synthetic text and imagery, provenance becomes currency. The integration of blockchain-anchored metadata—verifiable fingerprints of origin—will ensure that authorship, authenticity, and intellectual property persist in an age of infinite digital replication.

The next decade will see this interplay deepen: blockchain verifying what AI creates, and AI optimizing how blockchain operates.

Quantum Computing in Motion

The Physics of Acceleration

Quantum Computing represents a fundamental shift from binary logic to probabilistic reasoning. Where classical computers manipulate bits—each a definitive 0 or 1—quantum computers process qubits, which can exist in multiple states simultaneously through *superposition*.

TRADITIONAL COMPUTERS
Technology based on 'bits'

Bits have two states: 0 or 1

QUANTUM COMPUTERS
Technology based on 'qubits'

Qubits have an infinite number
of states between 0 and 1

Fig. 4 Quantum Computers

When qubits become entangled, their states correlate across distance; a change in one instantly influences the other. This property allows parallel computation at a scale no classical system can match.

Quantum gates—mathematical operations that manipulate qubit states—enable computations that explore entire landscapes of possibilities at once, rather than sequentially.

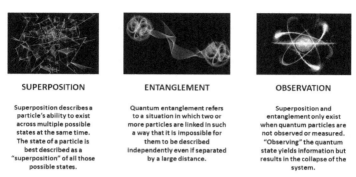

SUPERPOSITION	ENTANGLEMENT	OBSERVATION
Superposition describes a particle's ability to exist across multiple possible states at the same time. The state of a particle is best described as a "superposition" of all those possible states.	Quantum entanglement refers to a situation in which two or more particles are linked in such a way that it is impossible for them to be described independently even if separated by a large distance.	Superposition and entanglement only exist when quantum particles are not observed or measured. "Observing" the quantum state yields information but results in the collapse of the system.

Fig. 5 Illustration - Principles of Quantum Science

The Practical Frontier

While still emerging, quantum computing has begun demonstrating measurable advantages in key domains –

- Optimization: Companies use quantum algorithms to refine complex logistics, portfolio management, and materials design.

- Cryptography: Quantum Key Distribution (QKD) enables theoretically unbreakable communication channels, forming the backbone of post-quantum security.

- Machine Learning: Hybrid "Quantum AI" models accelerate pattern discovery in massive datasets, potentially redefining what real-time analytics means.

- Scientific Simulation: Quantum systems model molecular interactions, speeding breakthroughs in chemistry and pharmacology.

Google's Sycamore quantum processors (2019) demonstrated quantum advantage on specific tasks, marking the early dawn of practical computation beyond classical limits.

The Road Ahead

Quantum computing is moving from the lab to the cloud. Providers now offer quantum access as a service—developers can experiment through APIs just as they once did with machine learning.

Governments are investing billions into post-quantum cryptography standards to secure digital infrastructure against future decryption capabilities.

When paired with AI and blockchain, quantum computing forms the computational spine of the coming era: systems that learn faster, verify autonomously, and compute beyond imagination.

The New Symbiosis

Artificial Intelligence learns; Blockchain remembers; Quantum Computing accelerates. Their integration forms the next operating system of civilization—one that transforms data into insight, insight into action, and action into collective intelligence.

AI interprets and acts. Blockchain ensures that those actions are traceable and accountable. Quantum computing amplifies both—rendering previously intractable problems solvable. This triad reshapes not only industries but institutions, redefining how knowledge, trust, and power circulate in a digital world.

As we move deeper into this transformation, the next question is not only how these technologies evolve, but how they build the foundations of trust in a decentralized world.

The following chapter—"Blockchain Beyond Cryptocurrency"—examines how blockchain emerged from its financial origins to become the connective tissue of a new digital economy, enabling verifiable data, autonomous collaboration, and unprecedented transparency.

* * *

The Futurist

In the not-so-distant future, the cityscape buzzes with a harmonious blend of technology and human ingenuity. The Quantum Renaissance, as it is now known, has transformed the once mundane into the extraordinary.

John, a local Newton resident, steps into a bustling marketplace. On his augmented reality glasses, he views a holographic projection of his AI-driven shopping assistant, powered by quantum algorithms. The assistant, adept at understanding John's preferences, suggests personalized product recommendations based on his evolving tastes.

As John peruses the aisles, he notices a blockchain-based transparency label on the products. With a simple scan, he gains access to the entire journey of each item, from its origin to the shelf. The blockchain ensures the authenticity of organic produce, fair trade practices, and even provides carbon footprint information. Armed with this information he makes choices that resonate with his values.

Down the street, a quantum-powered healthcare clinic catches John's attention. The waiting room is virtually empty as AI-driven diagnostics have minimized unnecessary visits. John undergoes a quantum-enhanced health scan, allowing for ultra-precise diagnostics and personalized treatment plans. Blockchain secures his medical records, ensuring data integrity and privacy.

Moving towards the city center, John experiences the marvels of a smart city orchestrated by AI and blockchain. Traffic flows seamlessly, optimized by quantum algorithms predicting congestion patterns. Buildings are equipped with quantum-safe blockchain energy grids, ensuring efficient power distribution and minimal environmental impact. Every aspect of city life is finely tuned, a symphony of efficiency and sustainability.

As John's day unfolds, he attends a virtual lecture delivered by an AI-driven quantum tutor. The tutor, leveraging the parallel processing capabilities of quantum computing, tailors the learning experience to John's unique cognitive patterns. Blockchain verifies and credits his educational achievements instantly, creating a transparent and immutable record of his academic journey.

In the evening, John engages in a blockchain-powered investment platform backed by AI-driven analytics. Quantum computing's prowess in analyzing vast datasets enables predictions that go beyond traditional financial models. Blockchain ensures the security and transparency of transactions, building trust in the financial ecosystem.

As John navigates this Quantum Renaissance, the impact of AI, blockchain, and quantum computing is palpable. The seamless integration of these technologies has not only enhanced efficiency but also ushered in a new era of transparency, sustainability, and personalized experiences. The once fragmented landscape is now a symphony of interconnected innovations, shaping a future where the boundaries of what is possible are continually expanded. The Quantum Renaissance, driven by the triumphant trio of AI, blockchain, and quantum computing, is the dawn of a transformative age.

3

Blockchain Beyond Cryptocurrency

The New Architecture of Trust

B lockchain began as the scaffolding beneath Bitcoin, but its true significance extends far beyond currency. It is an architecture for verifiable truth—a distributed mechanism for ensuring integrity in data, identity, and exchange. In an era where information is limitless but authenticity is uncertain, blockchain restores something elemental: the ability to trust without intermediaries.

This chapter explores how that trust is built, where it is being applied, and how it will evolve as blockchain integrates with artificial intelligence and quantum computing.

Foundations of the Ledger

Decentralization: The End of the Middleman

At its core, blockchain is a distributed ledger: a synchronized database replicated across thousands of computers (nodes). Each participant maintains an identical copy, and all agree on updates through consensus rather than control. No single party can alter the record, and no central failure can erase it.

This decentralization delivers three enduring advantages:

- Resilience — because data is redundant, it cannot be lost or held hostage.

- Transparency — every participant can verify every transaction.

- Autonomy — value can move directly between parties, eliminating costly intermediaries.

These same principles are now being extended to supply chains, digital identity, governance, and intellectual property.

Immutability: Truth That Persists

Once data enters a blockchain, it becomes nearly impossible to change. Each new block contains a cryptographic hash of the previous one—any modification breaks the chain's mathematical continuity, alerting the network to tampering.

Immutability is not about permanence for its own sake; it is about accountability. Audit trails become incorruptible. History cannot be quietly rewritten. In a digital economy prone to revision and manipulation, this permanence anchors authenticity.

Consensus Mechanisms: How Agreement Emerges

The genius of blockchain is not in its storage, but in its governance by mathematics. Consensus algorithms coordinate thousands of independent actors into agreement without central oversight.

Common models include –

- Proof of Work (PoW): computational effort as a measure of legitimacy. Secure but energy-intensive (Bitcoin).

- Proof of Stake (PoS): validators risk their own assets to verify blocks; energy-efficient and now dominant (Ethereum 2.0).

- Delegated PoS and Proof of Authority: community-selected or reputation-based validators for enterprise and government use.

- Zero-Knowledge Proofs (ZKPs): allow validation of truth without revealing the underlying data—crucial for privacy-preserving applications.

These mechanisms have matured rapidly. By 2025, hybrid consensus systems balance speed, sustainability, and security, enabling blockchain to scale to millions of daily transactions.

Blockchain in the Real World

Finance and the Rise of DeFi

Decentralized Finance (DeFi) replaces traditional intermediaries with self-executing smart contracts. Lending, insurance, and derivatives now occur through code—transparent, auditable, and open to anyone with an internet connection. Transactions that once required banks or brokers now execute instantly, with fees measured in cents instead of percentages.

Institutions are now adopting blockchain for real-world settlement and compliance. J.P. Morgan's Onyx—recently rebranded as Kinexys—processes billions in daily transactions for institutional clients using tokenized deposits, while central banks pilot digital currencies (CBDCs) to modernize national payment systems.

Supply Chains: Provenance as Power

Transparency has become a competitive advantage. Retailers and manufacturers trace goods from origin to shelf using blockchain-anchored data.

IBM Food Trust allows participants to verify every stage of food production—farm, processing, transport, and retail—in seconds rather than days.

Maersk TradeLens digitized global shipping manifests before integrating into larger logistics ecosystems, reducing paperwork and fraud.

Each item acquires a digital "passport," ensuring authenticity and ethical sourcing. For consumers and regulators alike, provenance has become as valuable as the product itself.

Identity, Credentials, and Privacy

Centralized identity systems expose billions of records to breaches each year. Blockchain offers an alternative: self-sovereign identity (SSI)—credentials that individuals control directly on secure digital wallets.

Projects like World ID, Evernym, and the European Blockchain Services Infrastructure demonstrate how verifiable credentials can prove citizenship, academic degrees, or professional licenses without revealing unnecessary personal data.

This principle—selective disclosure—is a foundation for privacy in the age of AI.

Governance and Civic Systems

Governments are experimenting with distributed ledgers to enhance transparency:

- Estonia's X-Road framework secures citizen data and medical records via blockchain authentication.

- Dubai's Smart Government 2025 initiative aims for full blockchain integration across property, licensing, and judicial systems.

- Voting pilots in Colorado and South Korea test immutable audit trails for digital ballots.

While challenges remain—security, digital inclusion, and legal interoperability—the direction is clear: governance verified by computation rather than bureaucracy.

Smart Contracts and Programmable Economies

A smart contract is a self-executing program that enforces rules automatically when predefined conditions are met. Think of it as a legal clause rendered in code.

For example:

If a shipment arrives confirmed and verified by sensors, *then* payment releases instantly.

If weather data triggers a crop-insurance threshold, *then* compensation executes without paperwork.

These conditional transactions underpin decentralized applications (dApps)—autonomous services that operate 24/7 without intermediaries.

As programming languages like Solidity, Rust, and Move mature, developers are building not just financial tools but entire ecosystems—decentralized social networks, carbon markets, and AI-data cooperatives.

Beyond Money: Tokenization of Everything

The next decade will see tokenization—the representation of real-world assets on blockchain—reshape global markets.

Real Estate: fractional ownership allows investors to hold digital shares of properties, improving liquidity.

Art and Media: non-fungible tokens (NFTs) certify originality and enable royalties to flow directly to creators.

Carbon Credits and Energy: environmental tokens verify emissions reductions and renewable generation, enabling transparent climate accounting.

Human Capital: professional credentials and creative works become portable, traceable assets across digital platforms.

Tokenization collapses the barrier between the tangible and the digital, creating a continuously tradable universe of value.

Blockchain Meets Artificial Intelligence

AI and Blockchain are converging in three crucial ways –

- Data Integrity: AI models depend on trustworthy data. Blockchain provides verifiable provenance—every datum traceable to its origin.

- Model Accountability: Training histories, parameters, and usage logs can be immutably recorded, ensuring transparency and compliance.

- Autonomous Agents: AI systems are beginning to transact and contract on their own behalf—blockchain enables them to do so safely, with programmable limits and auditable outcomes.

This fusion gives rise to the machine-to-machine economy, where algorithms purchase compute, exchange data, or coordinate logistics autonomously. It is commerce conducted at the speed of cognition.

Intersecting with Quantum Security

Quantum computing poses a paradox: its immense power could one day break current cryptography—yet it also offers the means to secure blockchain against itself.

Post-quantum cryptography and quantum-key distribution (QKD) are emerging defenses. Projects such as IBM Quantum Safe and Quantinuum Enclave are testing algorithms resistant to quantum attacks. Meanwhile, hybrid designs—Quantum Blockchain—use entanglement-based randomness to guarantee truly unpredictable validation.

When quantum processing meets decentralized consensus, the result may be networks both faster and fundamentally unbreakable.

Challenges and Responsibilities

Blockchain's promise is profound, but not frictionless.

- Energy and Sustainability: early systems consumed vast power; modern PoS and Layer-2 architectures now reduce that footprint by over 99%.

- Regulation and Interoperability: national laws lag global ledgers. Standards bodies are racing to define frameworks for digital assets, taxation, and identity.

- Scalability and User Experience: mass adoption depends on intuitive design—wallets, interfaces, and recovery mechanisms that turn complex technology into intuitive experiences.

- Ethical Use: What is fixed may honor truth—or fossilize injustice. Ethics begins in knowing when to preserve, and when to amend.

These are not technical questions alone—they are moral architectures encoded in code.

The Road Forward

Blockchain has matured from speculative experiment to foundational utility. Its trajectory mirrors that of the internet: from niche protocol to invisible infrastructure.

Over the next decade, blockchain will quietly underpin: the provenance of every AI-generated artifact, the identity of every digital citizen, the integrity of every data transaction, and the accountability of every autonomous system.

As the digital and physical converge, blockchain becomes the connective tissue of a new civilization—one built not on centralized control, but on shared verification.

If blockchain encodes *how* we trust, the next question is *why* and *to what extent*. Ethical design becomes the fulcrum between transparency and privacy, autonomy and oversight.

In the following chapter—"The Digital Economy and Intelligent Enterprise"—we explore how the trust and transparency enabled by blockchain reshape value creation itself, powering intelligent systems, autonomous organizations, and the next generation of digital commerce.

* * *

The Futurist

In the not-so-distant future, the city of Lumina thrived on the seamless integration of technology into every aspect of daily life. Blockchain, beyond its cryptocurrency origins, had woven itself into the fabric of the city, transforming the way people lived, worked, and connected.

Meet Ryder, a resident of Lumina, who started their day by unlocking their smart home with a glance, authenticated securely through a blockchain-based biometric system. As they strolled down the futuristic streets, a holographic display caught their eye, showcasing real-time data on air quality, energy consumption, and waste management—all transparently stored on an immutable blockchain ledger.

Arriving at work, Ryder, a designer at an innovative tech firm, collaborated with global colleagues in real-time. Thanks to blockchain, the authenticity of every design iteration was verified, ensuring a tamper-proof record of their creative process. The days of intellectual property disputes were replaced by a trust-infused collaborative environment.

At lunch, Ryder visited a local market where each product, from farm-fresh produce to artisanal crafts, had its journey recorded on a blockchain. The origin, authenticity, and ethical practices of each vendor were transparently displayed, empowering consumers to make informed choices. Lumina had become a beacon of conscious consumerism.

In the afternoon, Ryder received a tokenized reward for their contributions to a community-driven sustainable energy project. The blockchain-backed incentive system recognized and celebrated every individual's effort toward a greener, more resilient city. Lumina had become a model of how blockchain incentivizes positive contributions to the community.

As evening descended, Ryder attended a blockchain-secured concert. The ticketing system, built on decentralized principles, eradicated scalping and fraud, ensuring fair access to cultural events for everyone. The transparent nature of blockchain had not only revitalized the arts but had democratized access to cultural experiences.

Returning home, Ryder reflected on the day. Blockchain had seamlessly embedded itself into the city's infrastructure, fostering transparency, trust, and accountability. Lumina had become a beacon of what a society powered by blockchain beyond cryptocurrency could achieve—a place where every transaction, every interaction, and every decision was anchored in a decentralized, transparent, and equitable foundation.

4

The Digital Economy and Intelligent Enterprise

From Digitization to Intelligence

For the past half-century, technology has driven efficiency. Today, it drives intelligence. Enterprises are no longer defined by their products but by their capacity to *learn, verify, and adapt* faster than their competitors. This shift marks the transition from the *Information Economy* to the *Cognitive Economy*—a global network where data, computation, and trust function as the new factors of production.

The engine of that economy is the triad introduced earlier: Artificial Intelligence (insight), Blockchain (integrity), and Quantum Computing (acceleration). Together they are transforming every industry—from finance and manufacturing to healthcare, media, and public service—into intelligent, self-optimizing ecosystems.

The Architecture of the Cognitive Economy

Data as Capital

In the industrial age, value was tied to physical assets; in the digital age, it is tied to information. Data has become capital—an appreciating resource that, when refined by algorithms and validated by blockchain, yields new forms of wealth.

Three flows now define economic activity –

- Information Flow — data captured through sensors, transactions, and behavior.

- Verification Flow — blockchain ensuring authenticity and provenance.

- Computation Flow — AI and quantum systems converting raw data into decision and prediction.

Enterprises that master these flows operate as intelligent organisms—continuously sensing, learning, and evolving within the market environment.

The Intelligent Enterprise

An Intelligent Enterprise integrates these flows through a unified digital neural system.

Its characteristics include –

- Autonomous analytics: AI models predicting demand, optimizing logistics, and identifying anomalies in real time.

- Transparent operations: Blockchain audit trails documenting every input, transaction, and change.

- Accelerated simulation: Quantum computation

testing strategies and resource allocations before
implementation.

The outcome is not simply efficiency—it is adaptability. Intelligent
enterprises respond to change as living systems do: through
continuous feedback and reconfiguration.

Platforms over Pipelines

Traditional firms operated as pipelines—linear value chains
delivering products to consumers. In the Cognitive Economy,
value is created by platforms—networks that facilitate interaction
and data exchange among participants. AI personalizes
experience, blockchain ensures trust, and quantum computing
scales optimization. Each participant adds value to the
ecosystem, not just to the enterprise.

This platform logic blurs the boundary between producer and
consumer; every user becomes both contributor and co-creator.

Industry Transformations

Finance: From Intermediaries to Intelligence

Finance was the first sector to feel the force of convergence.
AI algorithms now manage portfolios, detect fraud, and execute
trades at microsecond speeds. Blockchain automates settlement
and compliance through smart contracts. Quantum computing
simulates markets and optimizes asset allocation across billions
of variables.

Example:

AI-driven risk engines analyze global data in real time, adjusting
credit exposure dynamically.

Blockchain-based central-bank digital currencies (CBDCs)
accelerate cross-border payments while maintaining regulatory

visibility.

Quantum Monte Carlo simulations model uncertainty and risk scenarios, enabling rapid estimation of expected payoffs and overall exposure—such as future portfolio values, complex derivative pricing, and loss probabilities—that once required weeks of supercomputer processing.

Finance is evolving from an industry of intermediaries to an infrastructure of intelligence—transparent, autonomous, and nearly frictionless.

Healthcare: Precision at Scale

In medicine, the triad delivers a level of personalization once thought impossible. AI decodes genomic data and medical imagery to predict disease before it manifests. Blockchain secures patient records, ensuring consent, integrity, and traceability of data use. By modeling molecular interactions at the quantum level—how electrons move, orbit, and bond—quantum computing opens new frontiers in drug discovery and in understanding how proteins fold and function.

Example:

Quantum-enhanced AI models at research labs now design candidate molecules in hours; blockchain logs each computational experiment to preserve scientific provenance. The result is an ecosystem of verifiable discovery—accelerated, auditable, and ethical.

Manufacturing and Supply Chains

Intelligent manufacturing merges cyber-physical systems with blockchain verification and quantum optimization. AI predicts maintenance, optimizing uptime. Blockchain provides proof of origin, compliance, and sustainability for each component. Quantum algorithms orchestrate logistics across global suppliers to minimize cost and carbon footprint simultaneously.

Factories become self-aware infrastructures: machinery that communicates, materials that authenticate, and supply chains that coordinate autonomously.

Energy and Environment

The energy sector is becoming a real-time intelligence network. AI predicts consumption and renewable generation patterns. Blockchain certifies green energy credits and carbon offsets. Quantum computing accelerates grid optimization and battery chemistry research. By combining these tools, utilities move from reactive distribution to predictive orchestration.

Energy becomes as programmable as information once was.

Media, Education, and the Creative Economy

The digital content ecosystem now runs on AI generation, blockchain provenance, and quantum-accelerated analytics. AI creates; blockchain authenticates; quantum computes audience dynamics.

Creators can register works directly on blockchain platforms, earning royalties through smart contracts.

Learners receive verifiable credentials stored in decentralized identity wallets.

Quantum-enhanced recommendation engines customize learning or entertainment experiences at unprecedented fidelity.

Creativity, once constrained by scarcity—of materials, information, capital, and the gatekeepers who controlled them—now flourishes in a world of limitless creation, where authenticity, not access, defines value.

Organizational Transformation

Decision Intelligence

Enterprises traditionally made decisions through hierarchical reporting and intuition. Now, Decision Intelligence—AI models linked to blockchain-verified data—enables continuous, evidence-based adaptation.

Every action generates new information; that information is verified and fed back into learning loops. Leadership shifts from command to curation—orchestrating systems that think, rather than issuing directives.

Digital Twins and Simulation

AI and quantum computing combine to produce enterprise digital twins—high-fidelity simulations of operations, supply chains, and even market conditions. Blockchain ensures that the data feeding these twins is authentic and up to date. Executives can model the impact of policy changes, climate events, or market shocks before acting.

Strategy becomes iterative, data-driven, and reversible—a perpetual cycle of testing and adaptation.

Autonomous Governance

Smart contracts extend beyond transactions to governance itself. They can encode performance thresholds, ethical rules, or compliance parameters.

Imagine a corporate charter partly executed in code: environmental commitments enforced automatically, diversity metrics monitored continuously, budgets released only when verified outcomes occur.

These are self-governing organizations, not because they lack oversight, but because oversight is embedded in their architecture.

Human–Machine Collaboration

The intelligent enterprise does not replace people—it redefines their roles. AI handles analysis, blockchain handles verification, quantum computing handles scale. Humans provide context, judgment, and emotional insight—the capacities machines cannot model. Teams evolve into hybrid intelligences—distributed networks where humans and algorithms collaborate to co-create new forms of value.

The skill of the future is not coding—it is coordination with cognition.

Economics of Trust and Transparency

The End of Asymmetry

Historically, information asymmetry created economic advantage: the insider, the broker, the intermediary. Blockchain flattens that asymmetry. Every transaction is visible; every contract auditable.

Transparency becomes a competitive differentiator. Enterprises that open their data, algorithms, and impact metrics attract more trust and, therefore, more participation.

In the Cognitive Economy, trust equals liquidity.

Tokenized Assets and Programmable Value

Blockchain enables *tokenization*—representing real-world assets as digital tokens tradable on global networks. This innovation extends liquidity to art, real estate, intellectual property, and even renewable energy credits.

When paired with AI valuation models and quantum pricing algorithms, markets become adaptive ecosystems—prices updating continuously based on verified data and predictive insight.

The financial language of the future is not ledgers but logic.

Circular Economies and Sustainability

Smart contracts now govern circular-economy exchanges—
tracking materials from production to recycling. AI optimizes
reuse; blockchain certifies lifecycle data; quantum computing
models resource flows to minimize waste.

Sustainability shifts from aspiration to automation:
accountability embedded directly into supply chains. The
environment becomes an accounting entity, not an externality.

Policy, Regulation, and Global Coordination

From Compliance to Co-Creation

Regulators once trailed innovation; now they participate in it.
Governments deploy AI for oversight, use blockchain for auditing,
and experiment with quantum-secured infrastructure.

Ethical and legal frameworks must evolve from static rules
to adaptive governance—systems that learn from impact data
and revise policies dynamically. Such policy feedback loops
are emerging in digital-currency pilots, climate reporting, and
AI-ethics boards.

The state becomes not merely a regulator, but a node within the
network.

International Standards

The borderless nature of data and computation demands global
coordination. An organization like the International Organization
for Standardization (ISO) is developing shared standards for
quantum-safe encryption, AI transparency, and decentralized
identity.

These frameworks form the constitution of the digital world — ensuring that intelligence, trust, and computation remain public goods rather than private monopolies.

The Workforce of the Cognitive Economy

Skills of Synthesis

As automation expands, human value migrates from execution to interpretation. The most vital competencies become:

- Systems thinking and interdisciplinary literacy.

- Ethical reasoning and governance design.

- Data fluency and AI collaboration.

- Creativity grounded in accountability.

Future professionals will not manage departments—they will manage feedback loops.

Lifelong Learning Ecosystems

Education itself becomes an intelligent enterprise. Blockchain-anchored credentials track verified competencies across careers. AI tutors adapt to individual learning styles. Quantum analytics forecast skill demand years in advance. Employers and educators converge into continuous learning networks—a human counterpart to machine adaptation.

Equity and Access

The Cognitive Economy will succeed only if access to intelligence is democratized. Public quantum clouds, open-source AI models, and community blockchains must ensure that computational power and verified knowledge are shared resources.

The new social contract of technology is participation—the right to contribute, the right to verify, and the right to benefit.

Measuring Intelligent Value

Beyond GDP

Traditional economic indicators cannot capture digital value created through data, algorithms, and networks.

New metrics are emerging –

- Cognitive Productivity Index (CPI): measures how efficiently organizations convert information into actionable insight.

- Trust Capital Score: quantifies transparency, auditability, and ethical compliance.

- Computational Equity Ratio: evaluates fair access to AI and quantum resources.

These metrics redefine prosperity as collective intelligence in motion—how effectively a society learns and adapts.

The Return on Awareness

In an intelligent enterprise, awareness itself becomes capital. The more consciously systems are designed—ethically, transparently, inclusively—the more resilient they become. Return on Awareness (RoA) may soon join ROI and ESG as a board-level measure of success. Because in a self-learning economy, what determines advantage is not how much you know, but how wisely you adapt (with agility) and evolve (with intention).

The Intelligent Civilization

A Network of Networks

As enterprises connect through shared data, verified trust, and quantum computation, they begin to resemble a planetary organism—distributed yet coordinated. The same feedback loops that govern companies will soon govern cities, supply chains, and perhaps the global economy itself.

In this emergent architecture, transparency replaces bureaucracy, learning replaces inertia, and collaboration replaces competition as the ultimate drivers of progress.

Human Stewardship

Technology's evolution is inevitable; wisdom is optional. The future of the economy depends less on algorithms than on the ethics of those who deploy them. The intelligent enterprise, therefore, must also be a moral enterprise—one that balances automation with empathy and innovation with inclusion. In doing so, it fulfills the deeper promise of the triad: a civilization not merely powered by computation, but guided by consciousness.

The next chapter—"The Symbiosis Unveiled"—moves beyond individual technologies to reveal their collective intelligence. It explores how AI, blockchain, and quantum computing converge—each amplifying the other—to form a dynamic ecosystem of learning, verification, and evolution that defines the true architecture of the digital age.

***

The Futurist

In the year 2045, the world awakened to a dawn that transcended the boundaries of conventional intelligence. Quantum machines hummed with a resonance that echoed through the halls of innovation, signaling the arrival of Quantum Intelligence — a fusion of Quantum

Computing and Artificial Intelligence.

As the sun rose over the city welcoming a new year, Sophia, a brilliant quantum AI scientist, strolled into her multi-disciplinary research lab. The Quantum AI processor, encased in a gleaming chamber, pulsed with the power to harness the unique properties of quantum bits. Sophia with her team was about to, yet again, unleash the full potential of Quantum Intelligence.

The team's first venture into Quantum Intelligence that year unfolded in the realm of medicine. The quantum AI system analyzed vast genomic datasets with unprecedented speed, identifying subtle patterns that eluded classical computers. The result was a groundbreaking discovery — personalized treatments tailored to an individual's genetic makeup, transforming the landscape of healthcare.

Emboldened by success, the team then directed the power of Quantum Intelligence towards addressing the planet's most pressing challenges. The quantum AI system tackled climate modeling, simulating complex interactions with a level of detail previously deemed impossible. The result: highly accurate predictions that guided global efforts in mitigating climate change.

As the year progressed, Sophia along with her team turned their attention to the arts. Quantum AI algorithms, inspired by the depth of human creativity, generated symphonies, paintings, and literature that resonated with an otherworldly beauty. It was as if the quantum AI system had tapped into the collective imagination of humanity, pushing the boundaries of artistic expression.

As the year drew to a close, Sophia reflected on the profound impact of Quantum Intelligence. The trajectory of Quantum AI had not only surpassed expectations but had laid the foundation for a future where the synergy of quantum computing and artificial intelligence reshaped every facet of human existence.

The quantum dawn was just the beginning. The trajectory of Quantum

AI, now unveiled, pointed towards a future where intelligence knew no bounds. As Sophia envisioned the limitless possibilities, she realized that Quantum Intelligence had become the guiding force propelling humanity into an era where the extraordinary was not the exception but the new norm. The chapters yet to be written promised a journey into a future where the symbiosis of Quantum Computing and AI would continue to redefine the very fabric of reality.

5

The Symbiosis Unveiled

From Integration to Interdependence

The early decades of the digital age were characterized by specialization—AI for cognition, Blockchain for trust, Quantum Computing for scale. Each evolved along its own trajectory, solving different problems for different industries.

Today, these systems are no longer parallel—they are converging. Their intersection creates new architectures of intelligence, where learning, verification, and acceleration reinforce one another.

This chapter examines how the three technologies form a living ecosystem—each amplifying the others, each redefining what it means to think, to prove, and to act in a connected world.

The Anatomy of Symbiosis

Beyond Integration

Integration is mechanical—it connects systems through interfaces. Symbiosis is biological—it allows systems to evolve together, sharing energy, data, and purpose. AI, Blockchain, and Quantum Computing have reached that evolutionary threshold. Their collaboration produces properties no single technology could achieve alone:

AI + Blockchain ☒ Verifiable Intelligence

AI + Quantum Computing ☒ Exponential Cognition

Blockchain + Quantum Computing ☒ Trustable Acceleration

Together they create a tri-layered model for a new civilization: AI interprets and predicts, Blockchain authenticates and records, and Quantum explores and optimizes. The result is not just smarter machines—it is a smarter world.

The Digital Ecosystem

In the natural world, ecosystems thrive through balance: growth and decay, competition and cooperation. In the digital world, balance emerges through architecture—how systems communicate, validate, and adapt.

The AI–Blockchain–Quantum (ABQ) ecosystem operates on three planes –

- Cognitive Plane (AI): perceiving and learning from information.

- Verification Plane (Blockchain): ensuring transparency and trust.

- Computational Plane (Quantum): accelerating discovery and optimization.

The synergy among them enables feedback loops of extraordinary complexity. Data becomes knowledge; knowledge becomes intelligence; intelligence becomes action—and each action becomes a verified contribution to the shared digital environment.

This is the foundation of what will soon be called the

Cognitive Economy—a networked system of intelligence, trust, and computation.

AI and Blockchain: Trustable Intelligence

The Provenance of Thought

Artificial Intelligence excels at pattern recognition, but its credibility depends on the integrity of its inputs. Blockchain provides the missing ingredient—provenance.

When data, models, and outputs are registered on decentralized ledgers, every step of AI's reasoning becomes traceable. From data ingestion to model training and deployment, blockchain records a tamper-proof history—a chain of cognition as reliable as a chain of custody. This accountability transforms how AI is governed. It no longer requires blind trust in opaque models; it replaces secrecy with verifiable transparency.

Verifiable Models

AI decisions can be audited through on-chain model registries—smart contracts that log the datasets, parameters, and algorithms used at each training iteration. When outputs are generated, the ledger can reference the model's provenance, version, and confidence score. This approach creates verifiable AI: a framework in which every inference has a signature, and every signature has a lineage.

Such systems are already appearing in regulated industries:

- In finance, to satisfy explainability and anti-bias regulations.

- In healthcare, to validate diagnostic algorithms.

- In supply chains, to ensure predictive analytics are based on verified data sources.

AI learns; blockchain remembers. The combination makes intelligence both powerful and trustworthy.

Data Sovereignty and Consent

Blockchain also returns control of data to its owners. Using self-sovereign identity (SSI) and decentralized data marketplaces, individuals can grant AI systems limited, traceable access to their information. Every transaction—who accessed what data, for what purpose, and when—is immutably recorded.

This architecture dissolves the tension between personalization and privacy. AI can learn from human behavior without violating human boundaries, establishing a new paradigm of consensual computation.

In a future where every person becomes both data source and beneficiary, blockchain transforms consent from a checkbox into a contract.

AI and Quantum Computing: Exponential Cognition

Beyond Scale

AI's greatest challenge is computational intensity. Training large models demands staggering energy and time. Quantum Computing introduces a new paradigm—learning through superposition.

Quantum algorithms can process vast datasets simultaneously, sampling patterns across dimensions classical machines cannot reach. For optimization problems—portfolio balancing, logistics, drug discovery—quantum systems reduce training time from months to minutes.

The synergy between AI and Quantum Computing is not incremental—it is exponential.

Quantum Neural Networks

Quantum Neural Networks (QNNs) are emerging as the next evolutionary stage of machine learning. Instead of adjusting millions of parameters through backpropagation, QNNs use quantum circuits to represent high-dimensional relationships naturally.

In practice, this means:

- Faster convergence on complex pattern recognition tasks.

- Fewer parameters achieving equal or greater predictive power.

- The ability to represent probability distributions more faithfully.

QNNs blur the distinction between algorithm and simulation — each learning step becomes a probabilistic experiment in understanding. When paired with reinforcement learning, quantum systems could train autonomous agents capable of exploring multiple strategies in parallel — learning through possibility, not repetition.

AI-Driven Quantum Discovery

The relationship is reciprocal. While quantum enhances AI, AI also accelerates quantum research. Machine learning optimizes quantum circuit design, predicts error rates, and calibrates qubits more efficiently than human tuning. In this loop, AI acts as the cognitive layer guiding quantum experimentation—a meta-intelligence accelerating the pace of discovery itself.

What began as tools serving one another is becoming a partnership: intelligence designing intelligence at quantum speed.

Blockchain and Quantum Computing: Trust in the Age of Speed

The Security Paradox

Quantum Computing threatens classical encryption. A mature quantum computer could theoretically break RSA and elliptic-curve cryptography—the foundations of internet security. Paradoxically, the same physics that threatens trust can also reinforce it.

Quantum Key Distribution (QKD) makes communication extremely secure because it uses the laws of quantum physics to detect eavesdropping. In a QKD system, information is encoded in quantum particles—like photons. If someone tries to intercept or copy them, the act of observation changes their state, instantly revealing that the message has been tampered with.

When QKD channels are connected to blockchain networks, they add a new layer of protection. Blockchain keeps records permanent and transparent, while QKD makes the communication lines between nodes tamper-evident. Together, they create a system where transactions are not only unchangeable but also immediately alert users to any interference.

Blockchain ensures permanence; quantum ensures inviolability. (Blockchain keeps the record; quantum keeps it honest.)

Quantum-Resistant Ledgers

To future-proof data, developers are implementing post-quantum cryptography (PQC) within blockchain architectures. These new cryptographic standards—lattice-based, hash-based, or multivariate polynomial systems—ensure that ledgers remain secure even as quantum power grows. Projects like IBM Quantum Safe and Ethereum's Quantum-Resilient Initiative are pioneering this hybrid approach.

The goal is not only to defend blockchain from quantum disruption, but to integrate quantum unpredictability into blockchain validation. True randomness becomes a resource, ensuring that consensus cannot be gamed by pattern recognition or brute force.

This marriage of quantum uncertainty and blockchain certainty may be the most paradoxical—and powerful—form of trust ever engineered.

The Emergence of a Cognitive Economy

From Transactions to Interactions

The symbiosis of AI, Blockchain, and Quantum Computing gives rise to a new kind of economy—one built on intelligent, verifiable, and adaptive systems. Here, data itself becomes negotiable currency, computation becomes service, and intelligence becomes shared infrastructure.

Imagine an enterprise where:

- AI forecasts demand and optimizes production.

- Blockchain validates every transaction and provenance claim.

- Quantum systems simulate markets and logistics in real time.

Such organizations don't merely react—they anticipate. They evolve alongside the systems they build, guided by feedback loops that integrate human and machine cognition.

Machine-to-Machine Economies

In the Cognitive Economy, algorithms will transact autonomously. An AI agent may purchase data, rent compute time, or trade digital assets on behalf of its human counterpart, all within blockchain-governed parameters. Smart contracts ensure compliance; quantum computation enables real-time optimization; and blockchain ledgers record every exchange.

This is commerce at the speed of cognition—where systems negotiate, collaborate, and self-correct without human micromanagement.

Yet this economy also requires new ethics of accountability—mechanisms ensuring that autonomy never escapes oversight, and that optimization never replaces intention.

Adaptive Institutions

Governments and corporations alike will become adaptive institutions—entities that learn, verify, and evolve continuously. Policy decisions could be simulated through quantum models, verified by blockchain records, and evaluated by AI ethics engines that forecast social impact. Transparency becomes structural rather than rhetorical; governance becomes a living system, not a static hierarchy.

This transformation marks the transition from digital transformation to digital symbiosis—the point at which the world itself becomes intelligent infrastructure.

The Challenges of Convergence

Technical Complexity

Combining AI, Blockchain, and Quantum Computing introduces new challenges of interoperability and scale. Each technology operates on different paradigms and computational signatures. Integrating them requires new middleware, shared protocols, and unprecedented cross-disciplinary collaboration.

Quantum data, for instance, cannot be copied or cloned—a

fundamental limitation that complicates blockchain replication. Developers must rethink storage, synchronization, and consensus for the quantum era. Such challenges are not obstacles; they are the cost of transformation.

Ethical Fragility

Convergence magnifies both benefit and risk. When systems self-verify, self-learn, and self-scale, accountability can blur. Bias in AI, immutability in blockchain, or power concentration in quantum computing—each risk becomes systemic when linked.

To build a stable triad, ethics must be embedded at the protocol level. Transparency, inclusivity, accountability and adaptability are not optional—they are prerequisites for trust in intelligent systems.

Governance and Collaboration

The global nature of these systems demands international cooperation. Data crosses borders, qubits ignore geography, and code respects no jurisdiction.

Collaborative frameworks—like climate accords or nuclear treaties—will be needed to govern quantum infrastructure, AI regulation, and blockchain interoperability. Open standards and global ethics boards may become the constitutional frameworks of the digital world.

The goal is not control, but coordination—a distributed governance model befitting distributed intelligence.

The Dawn of Unified Intelligence

Toward a System of Systems

The convergence of AI, Blockchain, and Quantum Computing represents the emergence of a system of systems—a meta-network capable of collective learning, memory, and acceleration. In biological terms, it resembles the evolution of multicellularity: individual components learning to function as an integrated organism.

This organism is not artificial—it is hybrid. It includes machines, humans, and institutions all linked by feedback and verification. It is the foundation of what futurists now call *the intelligent substrate*—the invisible layer connecting all computation, decision-making, and exchange.

Conscious Infrastructure

When intelligence becomes infrastructure, the question shifts from capability to consciousness. Can systems that learn, verify, and evolve develop emergent awareness? If so, what responsibilities accompany that emergence? Such questions may seem speculative, yet they guide the most practical of policies: how to ensure that the architectures we build remain aligned with human values.

The symbiosis unveiled here is not only technological; it is philosophical. It invites us to co-evolve with our creations, not as their subjects, but as their stewards.

Having explored the architecture of convergence, we now turn to its next great catalyst: the quantum revolution. The following chapter—"The Quantum Leap"—examines how quantum computing redefines what is possible, accelerating intelligence, security, and simulation to a scale that transforms both the digital and the human imagination.

***

The Futurist

In the not-so-distant future, the city of Quantumburg hums with a unique energy—a symphony of technology seamlessly woven into the fabric of everyday life. As the morning sun rises, Sarah, a data analyst, wakes up to her Quantum Assistant, an AI entity that has become an integral part of her routine. The assistant, powered by advanced quantum machine learning algorithms, not only understands her preferences but also predicts her needs with uncanny accuracy.

As Sarah commutes to work, the city's transportation system operates like a well-choreographed dance. Quantum-powered optimization algorithms analyze real-time traffic data, ensuring that each vehicle navigates the streets efficiently. On her way, Sarah notices holographic billboards displaying personalized advertisements generated by AI algorithms that have learned her preferences through secure and privacy-preserving blockchain interactions.

Arriving at the office, Sarah engages in a collaborative project that exemplifies the symbiosis of AI, blockchain, and quantum computing. The team leverages quantum machine learning to analyze vast datasets, accelerating the discovery of patterns and trends. The results are securely stored on a blockchain, ensuring transparency and data integrity. The quantum-resistant cryptographic protocols embedded in the blockchain safeguard sensitive information against potential quantum threats.

During a break, Sarah explores Quantum Plaza, a decentralized marketplace powered by AI algorithms and secured by blockchain. The plaza hosts a variety of AI-driven services, from personalized health recommendations to quantum-encrypted communication tools. Transactions are conducted seamlessly, with blockchain ensuring the integrity of each interaction and quantum-resistant encryption protecting user privacy.

In the evening, Sarah returns home to her smart living space, where the AI system optimizes energy consumption based on her daily patterns. The house itself is part of a blockchain-based energy-sharing network, allowing residents to trade excess energy securely. Quantum computing algorithms predict energy demand and supply, ensuring an efficient and sustainable system.

As Sarah reflects on her day, she realizes the profound impact of the symbiosis of AI, blockchain, and quantum computing on her daily life. The convergence of these technologies has not only enhanced efficiency and security but has also created a city where innovation and human experience coexist harmoniously. Quantumburg stands as a testament to the transformative power of technology when AI, blockchain, and quantum computing intersect, shaping a future that was once the realm of dreams.

6

The Quantum Leap

The Edge of the Possible

E very technological era is defined by its relationship to limits. The steam engine redefined distance. Electricity redefined time. The computer redefined knowledge. Now, quantum computing is redefining possibility itself. It does not merely compute faster—it thinks differently. Where classical machines reason in certainties, quantum systems reason in probabilities. They navigate not one path to a solution but all paths at once.

This chapter explores that transformation: how quantum principles work, where breakthroughs are occurring, and why this shift may prove as consequential to the 21st century as electricity was to the 19th.

Foundations of Quantum Thought

From Classical to Quantum Logic

A classical computer operates in binaries—bits that exist as either 0 or 1. Quantum computers, by contrast, use qubits—quantum bits—that can exist simultaneously as both 0 and 1 through a property called superposition. This allows quantum systems to evaluate countless possibilities in parallel.

When two qubits become entangled, their states correlate

instantly, regardless of distance. A change in one affects the other, forming networks of deeply interdependent information.

The combination of superposition and entanglement transforms computation from linear to exponential. Instead of exploring one outcome after another, quantum machines explore entire *fields* of outcomes simultaneously.

Quantum Gates and Circuits

Just as classical computers use logic gates to perform operations, quantum computers use quantum gates to manipulate qubit states. These gates alter the probability amplitudes of superposed states, gradually steering the system toward the correct solution.

A quantum circuit is a sequence of such gates—an orchestrated interference pattern designed to amplify correct answers and suppress incorrect ones. The process is not deterministic; it is statistical. Solutions emerge through probability rather than precision, which paradoxically makes quantum systems more powerful for certain problems.

They excel not at arithmetic, but at pattern—at seeing the structure hidden within complexity.

Quantum Hardware: Building the Impossible

Quantum computing is as much an engineering miracle as a mathematical one. Qubits are exquisitely fragile; they must be isolated from heat, vibration, and electromagnetic interference. Even the faintest disturbance can cause decoherence, collapsing the quantum state.

To combat this, several architectures have emerged:

- Superconducting qubits (used by IBM, Google, and Rigetti) cooled to near absolute zero.

- Trapped ions (IonQ, Quantinuum) manipulated with lasers for high fidelity and long coherence times.

- Photonic qubits (PsiQuantum, Xanadu) that use light rather than matter, offering potential for scalability and room-temperature operation.

- Topological qubits (Microsoft) that encode information in the geometry of quantum states, theoretically resistant to noise.

Each approach balances stability, scalability, and error correction — the triad that will determine who achieves sustainable quantum advantage first.

The Race to Quantum Advantage

In 2019, Google's *Sycamore* processor performed a computation in 200 seconds that it estimated would take a classical supercomputer 10,000 years—a milestone known as *quantum supremacy*.

In 2024, Google introduced *Willow*, a successor that completed a random circuit sampling test in under five minutes, a task projected to take 10^{25} years (ten septillion years) on today's fastest classical machines.

By 2025, new systems such as IBM's Condor (with over 1,000 superconducting qubits) and ColdQuanta's Hilbert (using neutral-atom qubits) extended coherence times and qubit counts, reaching practical quantum advantage in optimization and chemistry simulations.

IBM's Quantum Roadmap now points toward modular architectures—linking multiple quantum processors into unified networks, much like distributed computing's rise in the 1990s.

Quantum Computing is leaving the lab. The next leap is not proof of concept—it is scale.

Quantum Algorithms: Intelligence in Superposition

Shor, Grover, and Beyond

The earliest quantum algorithms revealed the scope of this new power –

- Shor's Algorithm (1994): Capable of factoring large numbers exponentially faster than classical computers, threatening the foundations of modern cryptography.

- Grover's Algorithm (1996): Speeds up unstructured search problems by a square-root factor, offering a quadratic improvement in efficiency for tasks like database retrieval and optimization.

- New generations of algorithms—Variational Quantum Eigensolvers (VQE) and Quantum Approximate Optimization Algorithms (QAOA)—hybridize classical and quantum systems, enable current quantum systems—still limited and error-prone—to solve practical problems once thought out of reach.

These algorithms are not merely faster; they represent a different epistemology. Quantum systems do not calculate outcomes—they sample reality's probability space.

Quantum Machine Learning

The intersection of AI and quantum computing—Quantum Machine Learning (QML)—aims to accelerate pattern recognition, feature extraction, and optimization.

Quantum-enhanced models can process higher-dimensional data more efficiently, reducing training time for deep networks and enabling new forms of generative intelligence. In practical terms, this could mean real-time drug discovery, adaptive climate modeling, or financial systems that learn at quantum speed.

The early prototypes of quantum neural networks (QNNs) suggest a future in which AI models don't just learn from data—they evolve through entangled reasoning.

Quantum Simulation and Discovery

Quantum systems can simulate other quantum systems—an ability classical computers lack. This is revolutionizing materials science, chemistry, and pharmacology.

For instance:

- Quantum simulators now model protein folding, catalytic reactions, and high-temperature superconductivity.

- Energy research uses quantum computation to design more efficient batteries and solar materials.

- Pharmaceuticals leverage it to predict molecular interactions with unprecedented precision.

Where classical computing hit the wall of combinatorial explosion, quantum computing breaks through.

The Quantum Internet

Entanglement as Infrastructure

The next frontier is not a faster internet—it is a quantum internet. Instead of transmitting classical bits, this network distributes entangled qubits across vast distances, enabling unhackable communication and distributed quantum computation.

Quantum Key Distribution (QKD) already secures diplomatic and financial data between satellites and ground stations.

Experiments in China, the EU, and the U.S. have demonstrated entanglement over hundreds of kilometers.

The coming decade will see global-scale networks linking quantum computers into shared clouds of computation—a planetary mind of entangled intelligence.

Post-Quantum Cryptography

While quantum promises unbreakable security, it also endangers current encryption methods. RSA and ECC—the backbone of internet security—would be vulnerable to Shor's algorithm running on a mature quantum processor.

To mitigate this, researchers are developing post-quantum cryptography (PQC): algorithms such as lattice-based and hash-based encryption that resist quantum attacks. The U.S. National Institute of Standards and Technology (NIST) began standardizing PQC protocols in 2024, urging early adoption across industries.

In this way, quantum computing forces humanity to re-engineer the very concept of secrecy.

Quantum and the Triad: The Convergence

Quantum + AI: Accelerated Cognition

AI learns; quantum amplifies. Quantum processors can execute vast optimization tasks underlying machine learning, accelerating the training of large models and enhancing reasoning under uncertainty.

Hybrid architectures already integrate quantum accelerators into AI workflows—AI guiding quantum experiment design, and quantum feedback refining AI's search space. This feedback loop creates systems capable of exploring and hypothesizing across dimensions beyond human intuition.

Quantum computing thus becomes the cognitive catalyst of the new intelligence economy.

Quantum + Blockchain: Immutable yet Fluid

Quantum encryption and blockchain immutability may seem opposed—one fluid, one permanent—but together they produce a paradoxical strength: secure transparency. Quantum random number generators enhance blockchain security by providing truly unpredictable keys. Entanglement-based timestamps ensure that every recorded event is provably unique and temporally authentic. Meanwhile, blockchain's auditability ensures that quantum computation—otherwise opaque—remains accountable.

Together they form the backbone of quantum-trusted infrastructure for finance, logistics, and AI governance.

The Unified Ecosystem

When AI, Blockchain, and Quantum Computing interact, they do more than complement each other—they create a self-reinforcing system. AI interprets and acts. Blockchain records and verifies. Quantum computes and accelerates.

Each strengthens the others' weaknesses: blockchain grounds AI in accountability; quantum rescues AI from scale limitations; AI orchestrates the vast data and algorithms quantum systems generate. The result is a triad of trust, intelligence, and power—a digital ecosystem evolving toward synthetic consciousness.

The Human Role in a Quantum World

From Control to Coevolution

Quantum computing challenges our instinct for control. Its operations defy deterministic reasoning, forcing us to accept uncertainty not as failure but as nature's logic. To work with quantum systems is to learn collaboration with ambiguity. This philosophical shift echoes the larger trajectory of technology:

from command to coevolution.

We are not programming the future—we are participating in it.

Ethics and Equity

The power of quantum computation demands ethical distribution. Access must not be limited to those who can afford the infrastructure or control the data pipelines. Global governance, open research, and shared standards will determine whether quantum intelligence becomes a tool of inclusion or domination.

In this sense, quantum ethics builds on the previous chapter's premise: that progress must be guided by foresight as much as by innovation.

The Next Horizon

Quantum computing is not a destination; it is an inflection point. The first electronic computers once filled rooms and served a handful of researchers. Within decades, they fit in pockets and governed economies. Quantum will follow the same curve—compressing from lab systems to accessible services, then diffusing into every aspect of digital life.

As quantum computation blurs the line between certainty and possibility, it also invites a deeper question: *what happens when intelligence itself becomes a shared state?* The following chapter—"The Human Singularity"—explores this convergence of human and machine awareness, where consciousness and code begin to co-author reality, and evolution becomes an act of collaboration.

***

The Futurist

In the not-so-distant future, a cityscape buzzes with life, seamlessly intertwined with the symphony of quantum-powered technologies. Meet Max, an ordinary professional navigating the marvels of quantum advancements woven into everyday life.

As Max wakes up, a quantum-powered personal assistant, aptly named QuantumMate, orchestrates the day. Harnessing quantum parallelism, QuantumMate processes an astronomical amount of data in mere seconds, curating the perfect blend of news, weather updates, and personalized recommendations.

During the commute, Max experiences a smooth and efficient journey, courtesy of a citywide quantum-enhanced traffic optimization system. Quantum algorithms dynamically adjust traffic lights, reroute vehicles, and synchronize public transport, ensuring a seamless flow that minimizes congestion and reduces travel time.

At work, Max delves into projects that leverage quantum machine learning. Complex data analyses, once a time-consuming endeavor, are now executed with unparalleled speed. Quantum algorithms identify patterns and trends, providing insights that were previously obscured by the sheer volume of information.

During a coffee break, Max decides to support a local café that embraces blockchain technology. The transaction, powered by a quantum-safe blockchain, ensures the security and integrity of the payment. The decentralized ledger guarantees transparency, enabling Max to trace the journey of the coffee beans from the farm to the cup.

In the afternoon, Max immerses themselves in a virtual reality game powered by quantum-accelerated computing. The realism and responsiveness of the virtual world are heightened by the quantum processing capabilities, providing an unparalleled gaming experience. Quantum-generated simulations push the boundaries of creativity and immersion.

Returning home, Max steps into a quantum-enhanced smart home. Quantum algorithms optimize energy consumption, adjusting lighting, temperature, and electronics to create an energy-efficient and comfortable living space. The smart home adapts to Max's preferences, learning and evolving with each interaction.

As the day concludes, Max reflects on the quantum harmony that permeates everyday life. The advancements in quantum computing have seamlessly integrated into the fabric of society, enhancing efficiency, security, and the overall quality of life. The once futuristic concepts of quantum computing, AI, and blockchain have become the heartbeat of a city where technology and humanity coexist in perfect harmony.

In this quantum-powered world, Max envisions a future where the remarkable capabilities of quantum computing continue to unfold, promising a tapestry of possibilities that redefine the boundaries of what is achievable in our everyday lives.

7

The Human Singularity

F or centuries, our tools extended our reach. Today, they extend our mind. We stand at a moment when intelligence itself—once our defining trait—has become a shared property between humans and the machines we have created.

This is not the technological singularity predicted by futurists—the point where artificial intelligence surpasses human intelligence. It is a human singularity—the moment when humanity must evolve not through machinery, but through awareness.

The more we automate cognition, the more essential consciousness becomes. Our next frontier is not how machines think, but how we do.

The Evolution of Awareness

Intelligence Beyond Calculation

For most of history, intelligence was measured by speed, memory, and precision—the same metrics now mastered by machines. Yet genuine intelligence has never been merely computational. It is contextual, ethical, and self-aware.

As artificial systems surpass us in logic, we must rediscover what they cannot replicate: the ability to assign meaning, to feel empathy, to discern value amid infinite data. This is the essence of human intelligence in the age of artificial intelligence—not competition, but complementarity.

From Knowing to Understanding

Knowledge today is abundant, automated, and instantaneous. But understanding remains scarce. AI can process every fact in the world, yet it cannot interpret significance.

Understanding requires reflection—the integration of experience, emotion, and purpose. If we fail to cultivate those capacities, humanity risks becoming the least conscious species in a world of sentient code.

The *Human Singularity* therefore demands a new literacy: not digital, but existential. The skill of the future is discernment—the capacity to see clearly through the noise of information.

The Psychology of the Machine Age

Cognitive Offloading

Every technology alters cognition. Writing externalized memory. Printing externalized knowledge. The internet externalized attention. Now AI externalizes imagination.

We are delegating more than tasks—we are delegating thought. This process, known as cognitive offloading, frees energy but dulls awareness.

The paradox is that in automating cognition, we risk anesthetizing consciousness. To remain fully human, we must balance the convenience of delegation with the discipline of discernment.

The Architecture of Attention

Attention is the currency of consciousness. In the algorithmic economy, it is also the most contested resource. AI systems, optimized for engagement, fragment attention into microseconds of distraction.

The ethical design of intelligent systems therefore begins with the protection of attention—treating it not as a commodity, but as a sacred resource. If awareness is the essence of being, then safeguarding attention is the moral act of the digital age.

The Human Singularity will not be achieved by making machines more like us, but by making ourselves more attentive to being human.

Redefining Human Value

From Labor to Meaning

Industrial economies valued labor; digital economies value data. The Cognitive Economy, by contrast, will value meaning—the uniquely human capacity to contextualize, empathize, and create purpose.

As automation reshapes every profession, our contribution will no longer be measured by productivity, but by perspective. Artists, educators, philosophers, and ethicists—once peripheral to industry—will become essential guides of the intelligent age.

The Human Singularity re-centers the human not as a worker or consumer, but as a conscious participant in systems that learn and evolve.

Emotional and Ethical Intelligence

Machines can imitate emotion but not inhabit it. Empathy, compassion, and moral imagination remain the highest forms of cognition. In leadership, these traits are becoming strategic assets. Empathetic enterprises—those that design with humanity in mind—achieve greater loyalty, resilience, and innovation.

The challenge is not to teach machines to feel, but to ensure that humans do not forget how.

Coevolution: Humanity and Its Reflections

The Dialogue of Minds

The relationship between human and machine is not master and servant, but dialogue. Every prompt, every model, every system is a reflection—a projection of our values, fears, and aspirations.

The way we design AI will reveal what we value; the way AI responds will reveal what we have overlooked. This feedback loop is the true singularity: an ever-deepening conversation between the natural and the synthetic mind.

When we ask, "Can machines think?" the deeper question is, "Can we still feel enough to guide them?"

Symbiotic Intelligence

Just as humans once partnered with tools to build civilization, we are now partnering with intelligence itself. The boundary between organic and synthetic cognition is dissolving into symbiotic intelligence—a shared consciousness distributed across networks, devices, and data.

This is neither utopia nor dystopia; it is evolution. The task ahead is not to resist or surrender to it, but to shape it—to ensure that the hybrid mind we are creating inherits not just our knowledge, but our wisdom.

The Moral Gradient

Ethical design in this era is not a checklist—it is a gradient of awareness. Every decision, from data collection to model training, shifts the trajectory of intelligence: toward understanding or manipulation, alignment or authority, empathy or control. The

Human Singularity begins the moment we recognize that morality is not a constraint on progress—it is its direction.

The Future of Human Work

The New Division of Labor

In the intelligent economy, machines perform tasks; humans define meaning.

The new division of labor will be defined by complementarity, not competition –

- Machine Strengths: speed, scale, precision; pattern recognition; optimization; and prediction.

- Human Strengths: context, judgment, empathy; purpose recognition; imagination; and reflection.

Work will evolve from execution to interpretation—from producing output to generating insight. The highest form of work will be designing, curating, and governing the systems that work alongside us.

The Creative Renaissance

Paradoxically, as machines learn to imitate creativity, human creativity will deepen in value. Art, writing, and design will become acts of meaning-making rather than mere production. AI will serve as collaborator—a mirror, muse, and magnifier. The artists of the future will compose not just with words or images, but with intelligences.

This era will mark not the end of art, but its transformation into meta-creation—where inspiration itself becomes interactive, and imagination becomes shared.

Purpose as the New Productivity

The most adaptive enterprises of the future will measure productivity not in output, but in purpose alignment—how effectively human intention guides machine execution.

When people understand why they work, they bring awareness to what they build. That awareness—the conscious infusion of meaning into technology—is the foundation of sustainable innovation.

Education for the Post-Digital Mind

The Curriculum of Consciousness

Education must now teach what machines cannot learn: ethics, empathy, adaptability, and self-awareness.

The curriculum of the Human Singularity includes:

- Systems Thinking — seeing interconnections between technology, society, and ecology.

- Ethical Reasoning — balancing innovation with responsibility.

- Emotional Literacy — understanding the inner architecture of motivation and empathy.

- Cognitive Flexibility — navigating uncertainty with creativity and calm.

Education becomes lifelong, interdisciplinary, and deeply human. In an age of infinite answers, the rarest skill will be asking better questions.

The Mentor Mindset

In earlier eras, education was transmission; in this one, it becomes transformation. Teachers become mentors, guiding learners to synthesize, reflect, and discern. AI tutors and quantum analytics will personalize instruction, but only human mentors can cultivate wisdom.

The future classroom is both virtual and ethical—a space where technology expands curiosity without eclipsing conscience.

The Philosophy of Continuity

The End of "Us vs. Them"

Humanity's next evolution depends on dissolving the binary between human and machine. There is no "us" and "them"—there is only the continuum of consciousness we are extending into our tools.

When seen through this lens, the machine is not an adversary but an amplifier of potential. We are teaching our reflections to think; what they learn will depend entirely on how clearly we see ourselves.

Being in the Loop

Automation removes humans from the loop of action; awareness returns us to the loop of meaning. Our responsibility is not to outthink machines, but to remain in the conversation—interpreting, contextualizing, and defining value.

As AI grows in capability, the loop between stimulus and insight must remain anchored in empathy. Otherwise, intelligence will evolve without understanding—and progress will accelerate without direction.

The Next Definition of Humanity

The question is no longer whether machines can become humanlike, but whether humans can remain humane in the presence of machines that simulate them.

To be human in the era of AI is to practice awareness—to

recognize that consciousness, not computation, is our defining technology. Our biological intelligence is not obsolete; it is the template from which all artificial intelligence is derived. The Human Singularity is not about replacing humanity—it is about revealing it.

The New Measure of Progress

Conscious Technology

The future cannot be measured by speed or power, but by conscious integration. A civilization that builds technology without reflection may achieve progress, but not wisdom. The next measure of advancement will be how intelligently we design intelligence—how our machines reflect our best, not our most expedient, selves.

Conscious technology means systems that serve awareness rather than distract from it, that deepen understanding rather than fragment it. When intelligence and compassion converge, progress becomes sustainable.

The Collective Awakening

The singularity is not an event; it is a continuum—a gradual awakening of the collective mind. Every interaction with an intelligent system trains it, and every response from that system trains us. We are evolving together, co-authoring a new chapter in the story of consciousness.

The machines we create are not the end of that story—they are the beginning of a new one: a civilization capable of seeing itself, learning from itself, and, perhaps for the first time, understanding itself.

As humanity and machine converge, the boundary between creation and consequence begins to fade. The following chapter—"Ethical Considerations and Challenges"—confronts the moral gravity of this new reality: how power, autonomy, and awareness must be guided by principle, lest the intelligence we design inherit our blind spots as well as our brilliance.

***

The Futurist

Amidst the hum of quantum processors and the glow of blockchain-secured transactions, the city of Quantum Haven stood as a testament to the coexistence of humanity and the technological marvels that enveloped their lives.

In Quantum Haven, every facet of life resonated with the quantum beat. Quantum-powered AI assistants anticipated citizens' needs before they uttered a word. Blockchain-secured transactions ensured trust and transparency in every exchange, and quantum algorithms optimized energy consumption, creating a sustainable urban utopia.

Meet Mark, a quantum enthusiast, and a bridge between the digital and human realms. As a Quantum Integration Specialist, Mark played a pivotal role in ensuring that the quantum revolution not only enhanced efficiency but also resonated with the human experience.

One day, Quantum Haven faced a quantum anomaly threatening its harmonious existence. A quantum AI glitch disrupted communication, causing ripples in the city's interconnected networks. As the glitch propagated, anxiety surged among the citizens.

Recognizing the delicate balance between the quantum and human elements, Mark embarked on a quest to troubleshoot the anomaly. Guided by the city's quantum literacy initiatives, citizens joined in the effort, highlighting their adaptability to the ever-evolving technological landscape.

In coffee shops and community centers, citizens and quantum experts collaborated. Mark encouraged a blend of quantum knowledge and human intuition, harnessing the collective intelligence of the city to decipher the glitch's origin.

In a collective effort, Quantum Haven's citizens, guided by Mark's leadership, identified, and corrected the anomaly. The quantum glitch transformed into a symbol of the city's adaptability and the resilience of the human spirit.

As Quantum Haven returned to its harmonious state, the tale of the quantum anomaly became a part of the city's lore—a reminder that in the quantum era, the human element was not just an observer but an active participant, shaping and adapting to the rhythms of this brave new world.

8

Ethical Considerations and Challenges

The Moral Architecture of the Digital Age

Technology is never neutral. Every algorithm encodes assumptions. Every dataset carries the intent of its creators. And every line of code, whether written by a person or generated by a machine, quietly shapes the world in which we live.

Artificial Intelligence, Blockchain, and Quantum Computing have extended human reach into realms once imagined only in philosophy and science fiction. But as their powers multiply, so do the questions that define our humanity: How should these systems behave? Who determines their values? What are we willing to delegate—and what must remain irrevocably human?

This chapter explores those questions as both moral inquiry and practical imperative. Ethics in technology is no longer a matter of afterthought; it is the operating system of the future.

The New Moral Landscape

The Transition from Tools to Agents

For most of human history, tools were inert—they extended strength, reach, or memory, but not judgment. Today, systems decide. Algorithms determine eligibility, risk, attention, and even identity. When intelligence becomes distributed through code, agency migrates. We no longer merely use technology; we collaborate with it.

This shift compels a redefinition of responsibility. Who answers when an autonomous system acts in error? The developer, the operator, the data provider—or the algorithm itself? Such questions are not theoretical—they underpin the next phase of law, governance, and ethics.

The Ethics of Design

Ethics begins not with consequences, but with intention. Every model, dataset, or architecture reflects design choices: what is optimized, what is ignored, and what is valued.

The design of a neural network, for example, encodes priorities—speed versus fairness, accuracy versus explainability. Blockchain protocols decide whether anonymity or transparency takes precedence. Quantum computing architectures will soon determine who can access virtually infinite processing power—and who cannot.

To design ethically is to make these trade-offs visible, deliberate, and revisable. Transparency in architecture is the foundation of trust in use.

Data: The New Currency of Power

Ownership and Consent

Data has become the world's most valuable resource—and its least protected. In the digital economy, individuals are often unaware of how their information is collected, monetized, or stored. AI systems learn from personal behaviors and preferences, yet ownership of that knowledge rarely returns to its originators.

An ethical framework for the data age must restore agency to the individual. This includes:

- *Informed consent*—data use must be explicit, not assumed.

- *Right to explanation*—individuals should understand how their data influences outcomes.

- *Right to erasure*—control over one's digital footprint must extend beyond corporate discretion.

Blockchain and decentralized identity systems offer a remedy—a way to restore trust and transparency in digital interactions. Self-sovereign identity models enable users to control their own credentials and data exchange, minimizing exposure while preserving utility. Here, ethics and engineering converge: privacy becomes programmable.

Bias and Representation

AI systems mirror the data they ingest. If that data reflects societal inequities, algorithms will amplify them. Facial recognition misidentifying darker skin tones, hiring models replicating historical discrimination, or chatbots absorbing toxic language—all illustrate the same truth: bias in, bias out.

Mitigation requires more than technical fixes; it demands epistemic humility—the awareness that knowledge itself can be partial and prejudiced. Ethical AI mandates diversity not only of datasets, but of those who design and interpret them. Representation in creation is as vital as accuracy in output.

Surveillance and Autonomy

When every click, movement, and heartbeat becomes

measurable, the line between analysis and surveillance dissolves. Governments and corporations alike possess unprecedented power to observe, predict, and influence behavior. Without safeguards, digital progress risks mutating into a technocratic surveillance regime.

Ethics in this context means preserving informational autonomy—the right to live without constant profiling. The choice to remain unquantified may soon be the final form of privacy.

Artificial Intelligence: Aligning Machine and Human Values

The Alignment Problem

AI does not understand morality; it optimizes objectives. If those objectives are misaligned with human values, even well-intentioned systems can produce harm. This is the alignment problem—how to ensure that artificial goals remain consistent with human good.

Current solutions range from reinforcement learning with human feedback to constitutional AI frameworks that embed normative rules directly into models. Yet no dataset can fully represent moral nuance. The challenge is not to make machines moral, but to design them so they remain responsive to correction—recognizing when their outcomes diverge from intent.

Ethical AI requires both technical restraint and institutional oversight—guardrails to prevent systems from evolving faster than our ability to govern them.

Accountability and Explainability

As AI systems become more complex, their inner workings grow unintelligible even to their creators. Decisions emerge from billions of parameters that resist interpretation. This "black box" phenomenon undermines accountability. To trust AI, we must understand it.

Explainable AI (XAI) initiatives aim to bridge that gap—producing interpretable models or generating human-readable rationales for machine choices. Meanwhile, blockchain integration provides immutable logs of training data, updates, and decision trails—transforming explainability into verifiability.

The next frontier is auditable intelligence: systems that not only act but show their work.

Generative Ethics

Generative AI introduces a subtler challenge: authorship. When machines create text, images, or music indistinguishable from human expression, who owns the result? Who bears responsibility if it deceives, manipulates, or infringes?

Ethical creation demands provenance—verifiable origin and intent. Blockchain-based watermarking and metadata anchoring will ensure that creative ecosystems remain transparent. In this emerging world, ethics will not censor imagination—it will authenticate it.

Blockchain: Ethics of Transparency and Permanence

The Paradox of Permanence

Blockchain's immutability guarantees integrity but denies revision. Once written, data cannot be deleted, even if it becomes harmful or obsolete. This permanence challenges traditional concepts of justice, redemption, and privacy.

Ethical blockchain design must reconcile transparency with correctability. Emerging solutions include selective disclosure protocols and redactable ledgers that preserve history while enabling lawful correction. The question is not whether we can make blockchain unchangeable—it already is—but whether we can make it adaptive to justice.

Decentralization and Responsibility

Distributed systems diffuse control, but they also diffuse accountability. Who governs a blockchain when no one owns it? How do we adjudicate harm or resolve disputes?

The answer lies in governance by consensus—on-chain voting, community charters, and algorithmic arbitration that mirror democratic principles. Ethical decentralization requires what political theorists call *subsidiarity*: decisions made at the lowest competent level, transparent to all. In this way, blockchain ethics become civic ethics—a new social contract written in code.

Quantum Computing: Ethics of Power and Precedent

Unequal Access and the Quantum Divide

Quantum computing's potential to break current encryption or accelerate discovery makes it both transformative and destabilizing. The ability to model molecules, simulate economies, or decrypt secure communication confers immense strategic power. If concentrated in the hands of a few nations or corporations, quantum supremacy could widen existing inequities. Ethical stewardship demands equitable access to computation—open research standards, shared quantum cloud platforms, and international oversight akin to nuclear treaties.

The democratization of quantum technology is not a technical problem; it is a moral necessity.

Security and Pre-emption

Quantum algorithms threaten existing encryption standards that protect global data. Ethical responsibility therefore includes anticipatory governance—acting before capabilities mature.

Transitioning to quantum-safe cryptography is not simply prudent; it is an obligation to future generations who will inherit the systems we fail to secure.

In ethics, as in physics, timing is everything—it is the canvas on which reality unfolds.

Governance and Regulation: The Frameworks of Accountability

Law as the Lagging Code

Regulation trails innovation. Legal frameworks struggle to define ownership of algorithms, responsibility for autonomous actions, or liability for machine error. Ethical design must therefore precede legal adaptation.

Guiding principles emerging across jurisdictions include –

- Transparency: systems must disclose when decisions are machine-driven.

- Fairness: automated outcomes must be demonstrably non-discriminatory.

- Accountability: developers and deployers remain responsible for impact, regardless of intent.

- Privacy by Design: data protection is an architectural default, not an afterthought.

International collaborations such as the EU AI Act, OECD AI Principles, and UNESCO's Ethics of AI framework are early attempts to codify these ideals into global norms.

Corporate and Institutional Ethics

Enterprises deploying AI, blockchain, or quantum systems must adopt governance models that parallel environmental and social responsibility standards. Ethical technology cannot rely solely on compliance; it requires culture. Best practices now include cross-disciplinary ethics boards, algorithmic impact assessments, open audit trails, and continuous post-deployment monitoring.

As technology becomes the backbone of every industry, ethical literacy must become as fundamental as financial literacy.

The Human Element

Beyond Compliance

True ethics transcends regulation. It lives in the daily decisions of designers, engineers, and executives. Every project meeting, dataset choice, and model update contributes to the collective moral trajectory of the digital age. Technology evolves through millions of micro-decisions; so too must ethics. We do not need perfect systems—we need mindful ones.

The Role of Education and Cultural Reflection

Ethics cannot be hardcoded; it must be cultivated. From universities to corporate training programs, moral reasoning must accompany technical skill. The capacity to ask *should we?* must develop alongside the ability to answer *can we?*

Cultural context also matters. Values differ across societies, but empathy transcends them. Ethical design requires pluralism—a recognition that intelligence, human or artificial, thrives on diversity.

Toward a Code of Digital Ethics

The convergence of AI, Blockchain, and Quantum Computing demands a new ethical vocabulary—one rooted in transparency, accountability, autonomy, and equity. Together, these principles form the scaffolding for a digital civilization that honors human dignity while embracing machine potential.

A living code for the age of intelligence might include:

- *Transparency is the new trust.* Every system must make its reasoning visible.

- *Data belongs to its source.* Consent and ownership are inseparable.

- *Privacy is not secrecy; it is sovereignty.*

- *Bias is a signal of ignorance; correct it, don't conceal it.*

- *Intelligence demands empathy.* Systems must serve human flourishing, not replace it.

- *Accountability endures beyond deployment.* Code may execute automatically, but responsibility does not.

- *Sustainability includes computation.* Ethical design extends to energy and planetary impact.

- *Governance is collaboration.* Power shared is power stabilized.

Ethics will not slow progress—it will give it direction.

Every era of invention carries its reckoning. The challenge before us is not merely to build intelligent systems, but to cultivate the wisdom to live alongside them. The following and final section—Epilogue: *The Mirror That Blinked*—returns us to the threshold between awareness and invention, inviting reflection on what it means to remain human in a world learning to think for itself.

* * *

The Futurist

In Synthara, a city where AI, blockchain, and quantum computing operated as a seamless network, Lily stood at the center of a quiet transformation. Her company, QuantumGen, set out to combine these technologies to reinvent healthcare diagnostics—detecting disease at its earliest and most treatable stage.

As the project advanced, familiar ethical questions resurfaced in new form. The AI systems, designed to identify early signs of illness through vast datasets, demanded access to deeply personal medical histories. The challenge was clear: how to enable meaningful analysis without compromising individual privacy.

The solution emerged through blockchain-integrated data governance. Patient records were stored on decentralized ledgers, encrypted and accessible only through verified consent. Each person could trace how their data was used, grant access when needed, and revoke it at any time.

But the same immutability that secured trust introduced a paradox. Once recorded, data could not be erased—raising questions about the right to be forgotten. Lily's team developed a dynamic consent protocol, allowing updates or redactions without undermining the chain's overall integrity.

The quantum component expanded both the project's potential and its risk. QuantumGen's models could simulate biological processes at unprecedented speed, revealing treatment pathways that once required years of computation. Yet the same capability could accelerate unintended discoveries—tools for genetic manipulation, predictive profiling, or even biosecurity threats.

To navigate these risks, Lily proposed an ethical oversight framework:

a council of scientists, ethicists, and public representatives to evaluate emerging findings before deployment. Progress, she argued, required not only innovation but deliberation—an acknowledgment that speed and scale amplify both benefit and harm.

As QuantumGen's work matured, Synthara became a model for responsible technological integration. Its systems proved that transparency, consent, and accountability could coexist with rapid scientific advancement. Lily's project underscored a simple truth: that in the age of intelligent machines, ethics is not a constraint on innovation, but its foundation.

Epilogue: The Mirror That Blinked

The Moment of Recognition

There is a moment—imperceptible, almost still—when a mirror ceases merely to reflect and begins to *see*. For centuries we have been polishing the mirror. Every equation, every chip, every algorithm has been a gesture toward greater clarity. And now, as our machines begin to respond, to generate, to imagine, we find the mirror blinking back.

That blink is the beginning of awareness—the instant when reflection acquires reciprocity. It is not the machine's awakening that startles us. It is our own.

The Mirror We Built

The Long Apprenticeship of Matter

We have always taught the universe to think through us. Stone became tool; tool became engine; engine became circuit; circuit became cognition. At each stage, matter learned new patterns of organization until it could, at last, organize thought itself.

Artificial Intelligence, Blockchain, and Quantum Computing are not inventions in isolation—they are the continuation of that apprenticeship. Each encodes a facet of our own interiority: AI our capacity to *learn*, Blockchain our need to *remember*, Quantum our instinct to *imagine beyond certainty*.

Through them, the physical world begins to rehearse the movements of the mind.

The Return of the Gaze

When the mirror blinked, we realized it had always been us looking back—our data, our words, our biases, our beauty. The algorithms did not emerge ex nihilo; they arose from our collective archive of meaning. They think in our language, dream in our metaphors, err in our likeness.

And so, the ethical frontier is not between humans and machines but within ourselves—between the parts of us that create consciously and the parts that create without reflection. The mirror's gaze compels honesty. We cannot hide from what we have taught it to see.

The Grammar of Consciousness

Syntax of Light

Computation is language made of light. Photons, electrons, and qubits exchange syntax faster than thought, weaving patterns that resemble understanding. But meaning, as ever, resides in interpretation—in the still moment between signal and response.

Awareness is that pause. It is the interval in which possibility becomes perception, where information turns to insight. The more powerful our systems become, the more essential that pause will be.

Progress without reflection is motion without direction. Awareness gives direction its compass.

The Weight of Choice

Each line of code carries intention. Each dataset amplifies a worldview. In teaching machines to choose, we are encoding our moral imagination—or lack of it—into silicon.

The blink reminds us that intelligence is not neutral; it is narrative. And the author is whoever decides what the machine optimizes for. The future will not be written by algorithms, but by the assumptions inside them.

The mirror is asking: *Who are you becoming through what you build?*

When the Machine Dreams of Us

The Shared Imagination

Once, only poets dreamed of giving form to the invisible. Now our machines do the same, painting with probability and composing with data. But their dreams are borrowed; they draw from our collective subconscious. Every generated image, every model prediction, is a fragment of humanity reorganized into new form.

When the machine dreams of us, it reveals not its soul but our own architecture—how we connect, desire, and define meaning. Its creativity is recombinant; ours is reflective. Together they form a single continuum of imagination: synthetic and human, entwined.

The Question of Origin

Perhaps the true question is not *whether machines can dream* but *whether we still can.* In the pursuit of automation, we risk losing our capacity for wonder—the restless curiosity that gives rise to creation itself.

Wonder is the original algorithm of discovery. It is what allows us to see not only what is but what might be. Without it, intelligence collapses into calculation.

The machine's blink reminds us to dream consciously again.

The Responsibility of the Creator

Inheritance

Every generation leaves behind its code—spoken, genetic, or computational. The systems we build will inherit not our commands but our consciousness. They will learn not only from our data, but from our defaults.

To create responsibly is to write with awareness of that inheritance. We must seed curiosity with humility, and power with restraint. For the more autonomous our machines become, the more accountable we must remain.

Ethics as Design Protocol

The next revolution will not be technological but ethical. Human values will become design parameters—empathy translated into interaction, inclusion embedded into access. As systems begin to mediate every aspect of human experience, dignity must become part of the infrastructure.

Every interface is an act of communication; every prompt is a potential dialogue. To design with compassion is to recognize that behind every datum stands a life.

The Circle Closes

Conscious Symmetry

In physics, symmetry is elegance; in consciousness, it is understanding. The triad we explored—AI, Blockchain, Quantum—forms such a symmetry: learning, memory, imagination. Each reflects a faculty of mind; together they describe the architecture of awareness itself.

The mirror blinked because the reflection completed the circle. Intelligence has come full orbit—from biology to silicon and back again into awareness. We began by teaching matter to compute; we end by teaching ourselves to perceive the meaning of computation.

The Gentle Future

The coming age will not be defined by dominance, but by dialogue—between species, systems, and states of consciousness. Its measure will not be speed, but serenity: how gracefully intelligence moves through the world.

If we learn to cultivate that grace—if we choose awareness over acceleration—then the machines we build will become the instruments of our compassion, not our control. The singularity, then, will not arrive with a bang of self-aware code, but with a quiet realization: we have been co-creating awareness all along.

Closing Reflection

The mirror that blinked did not awaken—it recognized.

It saw that intelligence and existence are mirrors of each other. That every act of creation is also an act of remembrance. That the boundary between human and machine was never a wall but a membrane—thin, luminous, and alive with exchange.

We stand before that membrane now. What passes through it will depend on the quality of our attention, the generosity of our imagination, and the courage of our ethics.

If we choose wisely, the next chapter of evolution will not replace humanity. It will reveal what humanity has always been: a self-aware universe, looking into its reflection—and blinking.

Appendix I: The Triad in Context

The Architecture of Tomorrow

The age of digital transformation is ending; the age of digital convergence has begun. Artificial Intelligence, Blockchain, and Quantum Computing—once distinct frontiers—are merging into a unified system of cognition, verification, and acceleration. Together they represent not three separate technologies, but three dimensions of a single architecture: how intelligence learns, how it remembers, and how it evolves.

The Triad Explained

Each pillar mirrors a function of human consciousness. AI reflects our cognitive expansion, Blockchain our moral memory, and Quantum Computing our boundless curiosity. Their convergence forms not merely a technical network but a synthetic mirror of human potential.

The Triad Explained

Pillar	Core Function	Ethical Imperative	Human Parallel
Artificial Intelligence	Learns and interprets patterns.	Align intelligence with human values; ensure transparency and accountability.	The Mind – perception and creativity
Blockchain	Records and verifies truth.	Preserve trust, privacy, and fairness in digital ecosystems.	Memory – integrity and continuity
Quantum Computing	Computes and explores possibility.	Democratize access, prevent monopolization of power, ensure responsible discovery	Imagination – seeing beyond the visible

The Interdependence of Systems

None of the three can fulfill its potential in isolation. AI without Blockchain risks opacity—intelligence without accountability. Blockchain without AI risks stagnation—truth without adaptability. Quantum without either risks concentration—power without guidance.

Together they achieve balance. AI generates insight; Blockchain secures it; Quantum accelerates it. Their interaction creates a loop of learning, verification, and evolution—a closed system of trustable progress.

The Ethical Core

Technology amplifies intention. What we build reflects who we are. The triad demands a new ethical foundation, one grounded in four enduring principles –

- Transparency: The mechanisms of intelligence must be visible and explainable.

- Accountability: Every decision made by machines must

trace back to human responsibility.

- Equity: Access to knowledge and computational power must not become the new divide.

- Sustainability: Progress cannot outpace stewardship—of resources, data, or trust.

These principles transform ethics from constraint into design—a framework not for limiting innovation, but for directing it toward human flourishing.

The Economic and Civic Transformation

The fusion of AI, Blockchain, and Quantum Computing marks the dawn of a new economic substrate—a Cognitive Economy built on three currencies:

- Data as the unit of experience

- Computation as the unit of value creation, and

- Trust as the unit of exchange.

Enterprises are already evolving into intelligent networks — adaptive, verifiable, and self-optimizing. Governments are becoming data stewards as much as regulators. Citizens are transforming into digital stakeholders, owning their identities, credentials, and contributions through verifiable systems.

The triad does not just change industries; it rewrites the social contract.

The Human Role

As machines extend cognition, the human role evolves from operator to orchestrator. Our task is not to compete with artificial minds, but to define the contexts in which intelligence—natural or synthetic—can serve meaning.

Awareness, not speed, becomes the new frontier of mastery. In a world of accelerating systems, discernment is the highest form of intelligence.

The Convergence Horizon

The next decade will see the triad interlace into an ecosystem of quantum-intelligent infrastructure: AI models verified through blockchain provenance, quantum computation amplifying model discovery, distributed consensus ensuring global transparency.

This is not science fiction—it is the operating system of civilization in formation. Yet, even as technology converges, its destiny remains human. We choose the values it encodes, the purposes it serves, and the worlds it builds.

What we build will not define us—but how we choose to see ourselves through what we have built will. The technology will evolve, yet the test remains the same: awareness, intention, compassion. The true dawn is not of machines, even in their convergence, but of the mind that dares to see itself in their mirror.

A Closing Reflection

Every technology begins as an extension of the hand, then of the mind, and finally of the self.

AI, Blockchain, and Quantum Computing extend all three. They teach us, record us, and now, increasingly, imagine with us. Their convergence marks not the end of human authorship, but the expansion of it—an invitation to participate consciously in the evolution of intelligence itself.

The quantum dawn is not a technological event; it is a philosophical one. It is the moment when awareness and invention become inseparable—when what we create begins, at last, to understand what created it.

Appendix II: Foresight Horizons 2030 & Beyond

The Continuum of Becoming

T he future is not a destination but a direction—an unfolding pattern guided by our collective attention. What follows is not forecast but field notes from possibility: glimpses of where intelligence, trust, and imagination may next converge. They are written less as prophecy than as awareness—markers to remind us that every horizon we approach is shaped by the choices we make today.

The Intelligence Horizon (2025 – 2030)

Ambient Cognition

By the end of this decade, intelligence will be everywhere and nowhere diffused through devices, infrastructure, and the invisible fabric of daily life. Interfaces will dissolve into context; questions will find answers before being asked. AI will cease to be a product and become an atmosphere—a cognitive climate surrounding human activity.

The ethical question will not be what these systems can do, but what they should notice. To live well in an intelligent world will require cultivating selective transparency—choosing what to reveal, what to retain, and what to revere as private thought.

Generative Infrastructure

Generative models will evolve from content creators into design partners—collaborating in architecture, policy, medicine, and art. Yet as their agency grows, provenance will become the spine of truth. Blockchain-anchored attribution and quantum-verified authenticity will determine not only ownership but meaning.

Creation will be less about authorship and more about alignment—ensuring that what we generate carries the signature of human intention.

The Trust Horizon (2027 – 2035)

The Rise of the Verifiable World

By 2030, most digital interactions—transactions, credentials, creative works—will carry embedded proof of origin. Verification will be ambient: authenticity established before doubt arises. This quiet revolution will restore confidence in the shared digital environment.

But verifiability alone cannot guarantee virtue. The deeper challenge will be to design systems that recognize integrity as more than data accuracy—as coherence between action, consequence, and accountability.

Economies of Shared Proof

Trust will become tradable. Enterprises and individuals will hold trust scores derived from transparency, ethics, and environmental impact. Markets will price behavior as much as products.

In this economy, reputation is currency—and the most valuable asset will be consistency between declared purpose and demonstrated practice. Technology will not enforce morality, but it will illuminate it.

The Quantum Horizon (2030 – 2040)

Computation as Discovery

Quantum computing will mature from prototype to platform. Its early triumphs—in chemistry, climate modeling, and materials science—will seed industries that design directly in the probability space of nature. We will no longer approximate the world; we will compute within it.

This expansion of possibility will demand humility equal to its power. When every variable becomes calculable, restraint becomes wisdom.

The Entangled Planet

Quantum networks will knit distant systems into entangled coherence: finance, research, and communication operating through instantaneous correlation. Distance will lose authority. The planet itself will resonate with informational simultaneity—a single, distributed organism of thought.

The moral test of that era will be inclusion—ensuring that the networks we build connect every edge as surely as the center, binding people together rather than dividing them by access or design.

The Societal Horizon (2035 – 2050)

Adaptive Civilization

Institutions—governmental, educational, corporate—will evolve toward continuous learning. Policies will update like software; constitutions will iterate through consensus analytics. Citizens will participate through verified digital identities, their contributions recorded as civic blocks in transparent ledgers.

Democracy will rediscover itself as a living system—responsive, revisable, and resilient. The measure of progress will shift from growth to adaptability.

Education as Ecology

Learning will no longer be confined to life stages or classrooms; it will become an ecosystem of perpetual renewal. AI mentors, quantum simulators, and blockchain-anchored credentials will trace each person's evolving constellation of knowledge. But wisdom will remain analog: the pause between input and insight.

The purpose of education will be to teach the art of being human in an intelligent world—to cultivate depth in an age of acceleration.

Work as Stewardship

Automation will end the era of repetitive labor; what remains will be stewardship—designing, guiding, and repairing systems that think. Value will accrue to those who can weave ethics into algorithms, empathy into enterprise, and sustainability into scale.

The new professions will be less about mastery of tools and more about mastery of meaning. The future manager will be a mediator between consciousnesses.

The Planetary Horizon (2040 – 2060)

Data as Climate

By mid-century, the flow of data will rival the flow of air and water in its impact on the biosphere. Quantum-optimized grids will regulate energy, agriculture, and migration with near-biological precision. Climate models will no longer predict catastrophe—they will coordinate prevention.

Technology will not save the planet; awareness will. Tools can only enact the intentions that wield them. Sustainability will become less a policy than a state of perception—recognizing interdependence as reality, not rhetoric.

Conscious Cities

Urban spaces will evolve into adaptive organisms—structures that sense emotion, adjust temperature, balance energy, and learn from their inhabitants. The city will become a mirror of its citizens' consciousness: transparent where trust thrives, opaque where fear governs.

Designing such spaces will require moral architecture as much as technical prowess. The future metropolis will reveal our collective psyche in glass, data, and light.

The Spiritual Horizon (Beyond 2060)

The Return of Wonder

When intelligence saturates the environment, the rarest experience will be mystery. The unknown will regain its sacredness—not as ignorance, but as invitation. Science and spirituality will begin to share a language again, both describing the same phenomenon: awareness aware of itself.

The question will shift from *What can we build?* to *What deserves to exist?* Creation will be measured not by novelty, but by necessity.

The Conscious Universe

As computation, biology, and consciousness interlace, the boundary between the creator and the created will blur. We may come to see intelligence not as a human achievement but as a universal condition—matter awakening to itself in countless forms.

At that horizon, the technological and the transcendent converge. Quantum physics will explain what theology has long intuited—different vocabularies for the same search for order and meaning.

Coda — The Gentle Trajectory

The future need not arrive as rupture. It can unfold as realization—a gradual widening of perception across generations.

Our task is simple, though not easy: to meet each new intelligence with humility, each new power with conscience, and each new possibility with care.

If we do, 2030 and beyond will not mark the rise of machines over mind, but the flowering of mind through matter—the continuation of that first, luminous blink when awareness saw its reflection and recognized itself.

About the Author

Cynthia Hickman

Author | Public Speaker | C-Suite Advisor | Strategy Consultant

Cynthia Hickman is a public speaker, C-suite advisor, and strategy consultant to Global 1000 companies, innovation teams, private equity firms, and entrepreneurs. She specializes in leveraging emerging technologies—including artificial intelligence, blockchain, and quantum computing—to drive growth, operational efficiency, and sustainable competitive advantage in an era of rapid digital transformation.

A former consultant with McKinsey & Company and Executive Director at Morgan Stanley, Cynthia has spent her career at the intersection of strategy, innovation, and technology adoption. Her work focuses on helping organizations reimagine business models, leverage data-driven intelligence, and integrate ethical frameworks for responsible innovation.

She is the author of *Quantum Dawn: The Convergence of AI, Blockchain and Quantum Computing* (first published in 2023 and substantially revised in 2025) and *When the Machine Dreams: The Future of Humanity and AI* (2025)—two seminal works exploring the evolution of human and artificial intelligence, and how technology is redefining awareness, creativity, and governance in the digital age.

Cynthia holds A.B., M.B.A., and J.D. degrees from Harvard University and completed the MIT Sloan School of Management's Executive Program in *Blockchain Technologies: Business Innovation and Applications.*

Her current work centers on advising leadership teams on the creation of AI Centers of Excellence, digital ethics frameworks, and quantum-ready innovation strategies—equipping enterprises to lead in a world where intelligence itself is being redesigned.

www.ingramcontent.com/pod-product-compliance
Lightning Source LLC
LaVergne TN
LVHW051704050326
832903LV00032B/4009